I'm thrilled you are a part of the community and I'm looking forward for lots of more fun & excitement!

Love & Blessings

Sandy

FOREWORD

Time is valuable. So, to make a 'long story short,' most of the stories in my 'Search for the ***Thingamajig in the Bible Belt and Beyond*'** have been shortened.
Sandrea

The 'Towers of Washington,' the Original by Nancy L. Rogers, with permission © 1993 depicting L-R: First United Methodist Church; The Cecil B. DeMille Building; Old Courthouse, now BHM County Library; and the First Presbyterian Church.

SANDREA SHANE DAVIS

A 'Jewish American Princess's' zany and delightful Quest for 'Peace of Mind' and Finding that Special 'Something'

IN SEARCH
OF THE
THINGAMAJIG

IN THE
BIBLE BELT AND BEYOND

*One who can laugh at oneself,
will never cease to be amused.*

ORIGINATING IN AND EXTRAPOLATED
FROM THE PAMLICO SCOOP
JOURNAL/ADVERTISER (1989 -1998)

Copyright © 1999 by *Funnier Than Fiction Press*
A Division of The Pamlico Scoop
"News Journal/Advertiser"

All Rights Reserved

Paperback Edition

Printed in the United States of America
Library of Congress Catalog Number: 98-093692
ISBN 0-9667852-0-7

SPECIAL CREDITS

Cover & Layout Design:
Phyllis Zawislak

Photos:
Jayne Laliberte
('Le Polite Paparazzi') — Front Cover;
Terry Gray — Back Cover
'Michaelangelo' Mike Bennett — Page Six

'Washington the Original' Art:
(Nancy Rogers, by permission from a ©1993 print)

Proofing Technicians & Word Processing:
Donna Bronson & W. Joe Davis, III

Computer & Software Consultants:
Lugene Worth & Dianna Williams
(Aides to the *Frustrated* over 'Rage' Maker 5.0)

Language Consultant: Marion Weichel
(*La Contessa de Las Mercedes*)

Line Sketches: Anthony Adam Weichel

Inspirational Mentorship: Norfleet Hodges

Mechanical Design:
Friends Publishers
(Washington, North Carolina)

Printer & Publishing Consultant:
Gilliland Printing
(Arkansas City, Kansas)

ABOUT THE AUTHOR

Sandrea Shane Davis was born in 1950 in the outlying Pittsburgh community of Braddock, but reared nearby in the heavily Jewish neighborhood of Squirrel Hill. Graduating from mighty Taylor-Allderdice High School, the Author blossomed into a devotee of the early 'flower child movement, and pilgrimaged that summer to the hippie meccas of New Mexico and California with her New York City *cousinette-in-adventure*.

Straw hatted Sandrea posing with middle daughter Hannah Ruth on Origin al Washington's Downtown Waterfront.

Always sensitive to cultural 'hot-spots,' Sandrea moved to Chapel Hill, NC, where she worked several years and then embarked on a solo sojourn to England, Holland, Germany, a kibbutz in Israel, Athens, Crete, and the little Greek Island of Ios, camping for a time above the crystal clear waters of the Mediterranean Sea in a picturesque and cozy cave.

After experiencing the diverse adventures of European travel, the Author returned Stateside only to be plagued with a non-fatal form of 'continental culture shock' defined by a new 'agey,' 'god-realized' state-of-mind.

The 'goddess' Sandrea, as she thought of herself, soon removed to Raleigh, NC, where she began regathering her mental wellness (most of it, anyway!), earned a degree from the agriculture and engineering land-grant college, North Carolina State, and 'hooked' herself a husband, in the process!

Now, a mom to a covey of youthful Davises, the author lives in the river community of Washington (the Original), NC, with her brood and that same lucky husband.

So, welcome to Sandrea's Wacky World of hilarious and insightful thoughts — A virtual lifetime of humorous observations, punctuated by a very special brand of whimsical poetic license that you won't soon forget.

CONTENTS

Foreword
Title Page
Copyright Page
Credits
About the Author
Contents
Publisher's Extra!
Preface

I. Mama Mia..19
Could It Be In Squirrel Hill
At The Spa With Ma
Chickie's Birdie

II. All in the Family..28
Marriott Menace
Can Too!
The Tooth 'Unfairy!'
Stolen Wish
A Steal!
Scoring
Fashionably Late
Car Bashing
Flunking
Whining
Enragement

III. Relatively Speaking....................................45
Closet Skeleton
Awful Men
Catskills

CONTENTS

IV. The Countess..56
    Mushroom Hunt
    World War II.
    What Is The Countess Wearing?
    Punchin' Publisher
    Missing!
    Tony's Time Table

V. Friends..66
    Oldies
    Neighbors
    Dreaming
    Not My Stuff!
    Zelma
    Writers Bert and Naomi
    Witchell's Woes

VI. Washington, the Original........................77
    Is It At Fu Sun?
    Quasieball
    Dong Ho
    Gangsters
    A New Cult?
    Turnage Tales
    Images
    Splittin'!

VII. Puttsying Around The Pamlico 92
    A Ferry Cruise
    Chef's Blend
    Ain'cha Glad?
    I, the Boss

In Search of the Thingamajig...

CONTENTS

VIII. Spanning The Globe 104
'Burke-avarious'
Kenya's Khadija
Arapahoe
Chief Elder

IX. War Stories 112
Captured Hero
Captain Hill
He Won WWII
Rude Bernadette!

X. General Hospital 121
UFO?
Dentist
Cry Baby
Back Cracker

XI. Hard Copy 128
Scandal
Luger Legend
Lost Colony?
Naked Truth

XII. Carolina Journal 137
The Maestro and Sam's Bull
Kay Currie's Fate
Nature's Timing
Melting Pot Family
Stirring up hornet's nest
Telulah

CONTENTS

Bargain Hunts
Busy Bea
Disp'hair

XIII. Oy, Vey! 149

Bar Mitzvah Bash
In the Passover?
Holy Cow!
Mizpah
Hanukkah Crasher

XIV. Animal Crackers 164

Scooter & The Sparrows
Tom's Goats
Where Oh Where
Christmas Critter
Poochie!
Poor Deer!

XV. Musical Notes..172

Bath'n Bath in Bath
Hilton Head
Tapping With Clicquot
Twilah Sisters
Jitterbug
Abe's Clone
The Rolling Trolls
In The Commode?

XVI. Sketching the Search............................186

In Search of the Thingamajig...

EXTRA!
From The Publisher

A portion of this book's profits will go toward two organizations the Author is establishing: One, called M.A.W. (Mother's Against Whining); a second, is called W.A. (Whiners Anonymous).

Your purchase of *Thingamajig,* therefore, with its array and diversity of real life humor will help Sandrea's Organizations reduce the negative side effects of whining, while assisting to rehabilitate chronic whiners.

Laugh Lines editor, Victor Williams, quotes Steve Allen as saying, "Nothing's as funny as the unintended humor of reality." Or, as Dr. Seuss once coined, "From here to there, from there to here, funny things are everywhere!"

Mirth, in fact, is often cited as God's recipe for good health. So, with your purchase of
Thingamajig,
be mindful that 'Laughter-R-Us.'

'Truth *is* funnier than fiction,'
and the truths in this small volume are assembled to provide a happy diversion from the

chilling reports which clutter much of today's global landscape.

You can deduce from a reading of Sandrea's autobiographical and biographical essays, why she has a reputation for being on the eccentric side.

See if the contents of this book won't brighten your world with refreshing bits of comic relief and ol' fashioned fun. We bet it will!

Making you laugh is the Author's *motif operandi.*

Bon voyage, and many chuckles along the way!

──────── Published by ────────
Funnier Than Fiction Press
1110 North Market Street, P. O. Box 1607
Washington, NC 27889

To order more copies write or call
The Pamlico Scoop
Tel (252) 946-1553
Fax (252) 946-5599
e-mail www.scoop@skantech

In Search of the Thingamajig...

PREFACE

In The Bible Belt?

I'm wondering myself! What's a nice 'Jewish Princess' from Squirrel Hill, doing searching for a 'Thingamajig' in the middle of the Bible Belt?

I could have puttsied to my heart's desire in New York's Big Apple, along California's Big Sur, amongst the sun-baked Yankees who winter in Miami Beach, or across the Atlantic Divide on the Greek Isles, 'neath the Parisian shadows of le Eiffel Tower, or along the mystic shores of the ancient Nile.

But, no. It's my lot and privilege to puttsy along the banks of the serene, sparkling waters of Eastern North Carolina's Pamlico River, upon which sits the nation's Original Washington, the first town in the Americas named for President George Washington, and from which the acclaimed Hollywood film producer, Cecil B. DeMille has his roots (and a building named for him, to boot!)

PREFACE

     Upon settling here from Raleigh, in the early '80's with a young and growing family, I observed that there was a church on every corner for sinners to repent of their gossip, but no tabloid to report the latest gossip. This could not continue! Thus, my husband, Joe, began to publish a tabloid called 'The Pamlico Scoop' (a Journal/Advertiser), out of which some of the vignettes of this collection were originally published. Born and bred a 'thingama-good ol' boy,' Joe found it expedient and politically correct to crown me Editoress of The Scoop.

     There is method to my madness, in my ubiquitous search for the thingamajig, so please bear with me.

It may make you laugh.
Or may make you sigh.
But I have tried hard,
Ne'er to make you cry.

     It's such an honor to share with my readers how the Bible Belt has affected my brain—or as my dear friend, Joyce Tucker quipped, "What brain?"

In Search of the Thingamajig...

PREFACE

'Truth is stranger than fiction,' and while the autobiographical and biographical sketches in this book are nonfiction, they are woven together by that most elusive semi-fictional *Thingamajig.*

My teenaged middle daughter, Hannah Ruth, tried to define the Thingamajig. "It's like a *doomaflachee* and it is hard to explain. You have to just use your imagination."

However you define it, I have learned that the aura of thingamajig-ism can be translated into many different languages:

In France,
    Thingama-wee-wee;
in England,
    Thingama-bobby;
in Siberia
    Thingama-woe;
in Italy,
    Thingama-jiggilo;
in Germany
    Thingama-Nazi;
in Russia
    Thingama-trotsky;

PREFACE

in China,
    Thingama-wong;
on Broadway
    Thingama-song;
in Israel,
    Thingama-Jew;
in Australia,
    The thingama-roo.

There... You get the drift. With a bit of creative effort, you can probably 'translate' a few 'thingies,' yourself, from other countries.

However, don't lose sight of the fact that a
    thingamajig,
by any other name, is still a
    Thingamajig!

Sanford Rosner, whose 'persona' reminds me of Kramer in the 'Seinfeld' series, once asked me, "Is this search of yours kind of like searching for the Holy Grail?" Enjoy your read, and see if you think so.

I dedicate these writings to all of my family, friends, and fans; to my funny Mom, who has always believed that I am capable of

In Search of the Thingamajig...

PREFACE

accomplishing most anything; to my husband, Joe, for his dedication and fine tuning of this effort; to my brother, Mike, who better read this book, having already published one of his own; to my superior sister, Sorah, who writes better than I, and to my Aunt-in-Law, Lib Ross, who tries unsuccessfully to keep me from getting into trouble in this small town, but does manage to get me out of trouble at times; to sister-in-law Donna Bronson for her timely labor in my 'novel' endeavor; and to good friend Elizabeth Love, for expecting extraordinary things from me, like to write a wacky and reader-friendly book. Plus, I'd like to acknowledge Clayton Earl Chapman Jr., an African/American, who has been 'adopted' by the Markarians, an elderly Euro/American couple. Clayton was a Tennis Champ at Washington High School and is a 'disabled' Vietnam Veteran, who has won awards for his remarkable art. He still draws when he is not sitting on the corner of Bonner and Eleventh Street, watching 'the town folks' go by.

Above all, I want to thank my merciful and most gracious Maker, whom I hope not to meet before my time.

CHAPTER I

Mama Mia!

Could it be Squirrel Hill?

Squirrel Hill is the section of Pittsburgh, Pennsylvania, where my mother, Betty Shane, now lives. She was born Bessie Finklestein, one of five children, to Hungarian and Russian immigrants. My Grandpa Morris was a hysterically funny fellow. He never ceased to

CHAPTER I

make everyone laugh, except for my Grandma Gussie. Curious about that, my mother asked Grandma why she never laughed at her husband's great humor. Gussie answered, "I would laugh too if the fool wasn't mine!"

When the family down-sized the name to 'Fink,' Bessie changed her name to 'Betty' and then married my Dad, Morris Shane. Dad was a gamblin' man, which made for regular problems in their marriage. Years later, I arrived into this world as the baby of our family. I was their last accident and fortunately, or perhaps unfortunately for some, abortion was not legal.

Even my name was an accident. I discovered that fact as I was applying for the drivers licence that I never got when I was 35 years of age. Never feeling like a 'plain' Sandra (no insult intended to others who go by that name), I was elated when I noticed the 'e' in Sandrea on my birth certificate, and called Mom to ask her why the 'e' was hidden from me all these years. {After all, if I had known, I could have had a lot more time to make something more grandiose of my life!} As

CHAPTER I

surprised as I, Mom exclaimed, "The hospital must have made a mistake!"

There were no bagel shops in Squirrel Hill in my mostly 'happy-go-lucky' growing-up years. Now, however, there is a bagel shop on every corner and several in-between, like the churches dotted plenteously throughout the Bible Belt in which I now live. My 'search for the thingamajig' always includes Squirrel Hill's best **'bagelramas,'** when I visit Mom.

My Mom is quite skeptical of my stupendous search, saying, "There're a lot more important things in this world than writing a book about searching for the thingamajig!" When I asked her if she even knew what it was, she announced, "I haven't had one in fourteen years!"

At the Spa with Ma

Mom used the 'death sympathy tactic' on her son-in-law, Joe, to let me go to the Lido

CHAPTER I

Spa in Miami Beach for a week. She begged, "I'm 82, and won't be here forever! Please let my daughter go!"

It worked!

I would go to the Lido Spa with Ma just to make her happy. I was not expecting to have a good time, but at least I could look for the enigmatic thingamajig while there.

My airplane to Florida took a nose dive, but thankfully, leveled off before I woke up. Twenty hours on Amtrak was the result of that nightmare:

That nose dive on the plane
Caused me to take a train.
Amtrak has a track
To get me there and back.
At least it's on the ground.
'Trains'portation that is sound!

It wasn't too boring on the train, since I brought my hillbilly friend, 'Lila,' (...she demanded that I not use her real name). Lila rarely ever travels and baked a batch of brownies for our long journey. She repeated

CHAPTER I

her husband as saying, "I thought you were going to a 'health' spa!"

When she ran to the dining car to obtain her game prize, she was scolded by an engineer for not wearing shoes. "You'll get your toes cut off between train cars!" She replied, "Forgive me, but I'm jus' a lil' ol' gal from the country!"

When we finally arrived in Miami, we met a Peruvian 'macho man,' John, who was sent by The Lido Spa to chauffeur us to our destination. While on our way in the van, I 'stuck my foot in my mouth' and blurted out, "I sure am glad that I married before I fell for a South American man." He replied, "What! You don't want a macho man?" I answered, "It's not that. It's their reputation of not being faithful husbands." He retorted, "Oh, you are too pretty to have to worry about that!" Did I melt and fall for that line? Most certainly not! But when another 'Latin lover' told me I was pretty that day, I told him, "It must be true, since 'two' men have told me that today!"

Then Lila was told by Rolondo, the Cuban bellhop, who carried her luggage, "You

In Search of the Thingamajig...

CHAPTER I

'giv-a' me the 'goose-a-bumps-a!'" She replied in the most Southern accent she could muster, "I sure do like them purty legs!" Her husband and his wife can rest assured the flirting stopped there. As you can imagine, the elderly Jewish ladies got a kick out of my Gentile hillbilly friend — and vice-versa.

After settling into a pampered routine at The Lido Spa, I would have forgotten all about my six young'uns and hubby in 'Nawth' Carolina, but Mom kept showing everyone, including our waiter, our family photographs.

Tony, our waiter from Argentina, was adored by everyone at our table. He was most attentive, delivering 'whatever' before we had to ask. When I told him that all the ladies at our table wanted husbands like him, he told us that he has been married three times. Mom suggested, "You must have killed them with kindness!"

Later, Mom introduced me to Terri Ross, the phenomenal Entertainment Director at the Lido, who brings in well-known singers and comedians. For live swing band night, she

CHAPTER I

recruited elderly gentlemen to dance with all the single ladies. Mom refused to dance with any of those Chippendales, saying, "Those men look like they have been embalmed." Soon, however, my 82-year-old Mom was enjoying 'cha-cha-ing' with a jolly one!

I was having too good of a time to remember my 'search.' Then, I met a Cabaret entertainer, whose name is Sandra Elaine. Mine is Sandrea Ellen — Instant connection! When Sandra told an elderly lady that we were soul mates, she exclaimed, "You're what? ...Cell mates?" We corrected her not. From then on, we were *cell mates in crime!*

Sandra insisted we go 'Latin' dancing at Mangos. I accepted in order to thingamajig-hunt at South Beach. We both are fairly well behaved — not drinkers, gamblers, smokers or manizers, and have more fun, as a result.

Sandra is the glamorous one of our duo and was asked to dance immediately. I was content being a wallflower and thinking about this tentative 'search' of mine. Then, one of her Cuban dance partners got tired of waiting for her and asked me to the dance floor. After the

CHAPTER I

fifth dance, he expressed to me the only three English words he knew... "I love you." I showed him my wedding ring and shouted, "Seis bambinos!" He shrugged his shoulders in a so-what' manner. I later asked Sandra if that Cuban told her that he loved her. I was flattered that he only told me that.

Thankfully, our karate-expert 'bodyguard' that we met near The Lido, rescued us. Mangos is a 'den' for the 'young and the reckless'... Not for the 'older and the wiser.' So, we ski-daddled!

I will be fortunate if my husband will let me go back, when he reads all about my adventures at The Lido Spa.

CHAPTER I

Chickie's Birdie

Ten years ago, Mom brought her 73 year old boyfriend, 'Chickie,' to visit us, the Davis family. He is a former boxer, used car salesman, and a 'bookie,' but that's beside the point.

My husband took him to Bayview Golf Course, alongside the Pamlico River. The surprised Chickie Aingeman stroked the ball with his nine iron 85 yards onto the ninth green and into the cup. The two rejoiced with shouts of amazement and were exceedingly glad.

Prior to this visit, Aingeman spent 30 days vacationing in Miami Beach. However, he will always have fonder memories of Bayview, since that is where he saw his very first 'birdie.'

Chickie is still ticking at 83 and is Mom's weekly dinner guest, enthralled with her Jewish penicillin, (chicken noodle soup). Mom refused his offers of 'marital bliss,' saying, "One man was enough to take care of!" But Chickie has been a great 'daddy' figure for me and my siblings, even though he hasn't been able to help me in my relentless search for the Thingamajig.

In Search of the Thingamajig...

CHAPTER II

All in the Family

##

Marriott Menace

When my youngest child, Joseph, was five, he looked exactly like the child actor who played in the movie, 'Dennis the Menace.' Worse than that, his behavior wasn't much better. After a week at The Greentree Marriott in Pittsburgh, life there has never been the same.

CHAPTER II

Joseph's notorious hyperactivities raised many an eyebrow, especially those of a most pleasantly dispositioned shoe shine man. Joseph was yelling his head off in the elevator after getting stuck. The shoe shine man shouted at him gleefully, "At last you are contained. I told you not to play on the elevator! Didn't I?"

The Inn's management insisted on rescuing the 'little rascal' over strong protests.

The next day, Joseph turned up missing. Was he *menace-napped*? (A job, no doubt, fraught with perils your average kidnapper might not have considered!) In any case, our little 'man' was nowhere to be found. We searched the Hotel high and low — but, to no avail. We wondered, "Did that nice shoe shine man do away with 'Joseph the Menace?'" As it turned out, our little fellow *was* 'napped.' He was found taking a 'nap' in a corner by a door in the Hotel's Grand Ballroom.

In the 'Inn,' keeping up with the whereabouts of my 'little darling' proved too time-consuming to search for the thingamajig. As we checked out, I was almost certain I heard muffled refrains of rejoicing. 'Little' wonder!

In Search of the Thingamajig...

CHAPTER II

an, Too!

Who says white boys can't jump? When Joseph was eight, he was the only white boy on the Boys and Girls Club summer league basketball teams. After he was disciplined by his coach for talking and not listening (a family curse inherited from his daddy), his Coach, John Cantrell, was forced to beg the Club leader to make an exception to allow Joseph back on the team to play in the championship game.

As the championship game wound down, Joseph hit a turnaround to put his team in an 11 to 11 tie. Then, with but seconds remaining, he rattled home a game-preserving three-pointer.

Meanwhile, Joseph had scored 13 of the 17 points registered by his team. Immediately after the final buzzer, some of the players in the older league gave blue-eyed, blond-haired Joseph a victory ride upon their shoulders around the court in great celebration. Jump'n Joe had won their respect — and, yes, white boys can, too, jump.

CHAPTER II

The Tooth 'Unfair-y!'

As I was searching around the house for the thingamajig one day, I heard the kids discussing the Tooth 'Unfair-y.' Since I thought Hannah's version sounded so cute, I asked her to write the details of her discussion.

Here's Hannah's commentary about the tooth fairy, when she was around eleven:

People may call him the Tooth Fairy, but he is really the Tooth 'Unfair-y.' Rebekah and I were trying to convince our younger brother, Joseph, who had just lost his tooth, that there really was a Tooth Fairy. As we were talking, we got into discussing how much the Tooth Fairy had given each of us. I said he gave me one dollar for each tooth I lost until I was nine years old. Then he didn't give me anything. Rebekah said he only gave her fifty cents for each tooth, but he still gives her money and she is ten years old. Poor Joseph! He has lost four teeth and still has not gotten a penny from that Tooth 'Unfair-y,' which pretty much explains why we call him what we call him.

In Search of the Thingamajig...

CHAPTER II

Author's note: Speaking of William Jefferson Clinton, Hannah recently exclaimed, "I can't believe the President can commit 'purgatory' and get away with it!" She corrected herself after hearing her parents laugh.

S*tolen Wish*

When youngest daughter, Rebekah, was nine, I caught her 'cleaning' out a wishing well outside of The Oriental Marina Motel and Restaurant in Oriental, North Carolina. I shouted, "How can you just take those coins that people have made wishes with? Throw them back, right now!"

She replied, "But Mom... Wishes don't come true, anyway. I wished for $1,000 last year, and my wish never came true."

"The mouth of the South," as my Pittsburgh uncle Ralphy 'coined' Rebekah, I was persuaded by her heady plea and allowed her to keep the coins. On the way home she

CHAPTER II

told me it all added up to a dollar. I told her, "If you had just wished for a dollar last year, your wish would have come true!"

No matter, a fraction of her wish did come true, and right out of a wishing well. So, wish at your own risk, since your wishes may be stolen. There's no guarantee. Even my Mom's friend, Chickie, says, "You may as well wish for a million dollars. It won't cost a penny more!"

However, if you want your wish to come true, wish conservatively. And please wish that my search may have a successful ending. Wishing you 'well,' I remain vigilant in my search for the thingamajig!

CHAPTER II

A *steal!*

My second oldest girl, Elizabeth Tarah, was an All-Star on Emmanuel's basketball team. She had a lot of practice with her older brother and his little African American friends who'd come over and shoot on our backyard goal. But when she transferred to Washington High School she became a bench warmer, since she was only in the 10th grade. Finally, one game, the coach put her in. But nobody on her team would share the ball with her, so Tarah resorted to court thievery and stole the ball from an opposing player.

Weeks later the coach of the boy's team saw Tarah swishing her three-point shots and asked, "Why don't you score in a game?" to which she responded, "It's hard to score from the bench!"

CHAPTER II

coring

Yours truly and the other Moms played softball against our own flesh and blood, because Tarah's softball team at Emmanuel School challenged us. I actually scored one-half of all the runs for the Mom's team, when I accidentally bunted my way to first base, then slid to second, raced to third and then, leaped home.

Mrs. Bright scored the other half of our team's points. We should have been honored as MVP's, but since we lost 9 to 2, we got no respect... Maybe next year!

I did get something, however. Teased! Fellow team player, top educator, and super mom, Monica Burns, poked fun at me for leaving my lipstick on the table in the dug out. So much for vanity, as I put a *pretty* face on in my stressed, but determined, pursuit of that 'what-cha-ma-call-it.'

CHAPTER II

F ashionably Late

My oldest daughter, Abby, had her first date to the Prom with Carl Druhl, who not only has a persona similar to the movie star, Jim Carey, but can really put on a great 'Jim Carey' impersonation. When Carl arrived, he instructed Abby on the importance of being fashionably late. Carl would like to share that instruction with you:

"Fashionably late? I didn't know what it meant until I showed up for my first prom, eyes beaming, with date in hand. I was told that we were the first ones there and that it was not fashionable to be early. We quickly discovered what being fashionably late meant because for the next hour we had to entertain ourselves.

"Now that I am on my third prom and escorting another beautiful lady, experience has taught me a lesson I won't soon forget!"

CHAPTER II

Note: Carl is from Cary, North Carolina where his mom, Jennette Druhl Whitesell, and I met when Carl was a mere babe. We moved to Washington, where we live, now, but Jennette and family visit us regularly when I am not too busy searching.

On one visit when Carl and Abby were eight years old, Carl fell backwards through our second story window. Abby instantly grabbed the bottom of his legs and held on until her six-year-old sister, Tarah, helped her reel him back in. It wasn't enough for her to receive a reward from Carl's mom for saving her son's life, but down the road, just eight years later, Abby's still trying to collect on her reward — demanding a car, no less!

Such are the expectations of today's heroines. Save a life and expect a car!

CHAPTER II

*C*ar Bashing

I wish we had public transportation in the United States like the Europeans. It would be a lot more expedient for me and much more pleasant to search for that elusive thingamajig. I do not like cars and refuse to drive, although, I did try to learn once upon a time — only to get agitated, frustrated, and panicked. I had a driver's permit, but was alone driving when I left my car parked against a telephone pole down the block from my house. I exited the *stubborn* vehicle, and walked on home. When I did get home, my husband soon figured out that he'd have to go looking for the car, himself, since I was too 'clamed up' to tell him about my ordeal!

I'm a natural born *non-driver.* Even the shopping carts that I attempt to maneuver at Winn Dixie have been a hazard to fellow shoppers. If I must get somewhere, Hubby Joe, is my 'Joe-ffeur,' and I take full advantage of this form of transportation.

Abby, my oldest daughter at UNC — Asheville, accused me of being paranoid,

CHAPTER II

saying, "Just because you suffered by not driving your whole life, you want me to suffer and won't let Daddy buy me a car."

Let me make one point perfectly clear. I do fancy myself to be a most effective back seat driver, having survived almost half a century. I just really love it when my seventy-five year-old friend, Selma Stallings, looks right at me when she's talking while her car is moving. I immediately reprimand her, saying, "I hear you even when you are watching the road. So please don't be polite by looking at me as you converse!" Years ago, my husband, who has the same malady, almost ran into a tree when he turned to me to engage in chitchat while driving. In fact, he looks all over the place when he drives. I'd have thought that by now, with years of coaching from me, he'd have learned his lesson. It's a good thing I'm usually with him in the car to be an extra pair of eyes. So far, the two of us are wreck free, but not, *close-call* free!

It is well known that most auto accidents occur within twenty miles of one's home. Here's hoping we can sell our house and move at least twenty-five miles away!

CHAPTER II

Flunking

Flunking the ninth grade at Emmanuel was a jolt for my oldest son, Jesse, but apparently not enough of one. He narrowly escaped failing the twelfth grade at Washington High for not completing a required term paper. Sometimes Jesse just tried to skim his way by.

But, I must assume much of the blame. Most of his attitude was probably my fault. I never ever bugged him about doing his homework. I made him practice the piano an hour each day, as much to keep him from fighting with his sibling sisters, as for improving his playing ability. This discipline eventually paid off with an A. J. Fletcher scholarship to the North Carolina School of Performing Arts.

Jesse's love of music was inspired by Looney Tunes, and particularly by Bugs Bunny. As a kid, Jesse loved the classical music in the cartoons, as well as the animated characters that

CHAPTER II

seemed to be moved by the music of Bach, Mozart, Beethovan, and Chopin.

But I digress. A neighbor and former school superintendent, Gray Hodges, offered to do Jesse's term paper to make sure Jesse would pass. I told Gray that it would make a great front page story; "Former School Superintendent Saves Maestro From Flunking." He exclaimed, "Don't you dare. We'll both end up in trouble!"

Jesse did complete the paper, by himself, in the nick of time. He is in his fourth year of college and has won scholarships to study in Paris and Switzerland during the past summers.

There is a fiancee in the picture, who also is a grand pianist and most lovely. She refuses to change her last name after the wedding. Luckily, her name is Leslie Davis! When they perform together, they are known as Davis 'n Davis. Poor Leslie. I was too busy in my obsessive search for that elusive thingamajig to make Jesse clean up his room. But, then, they say that love conquers all, and Leslie probably doesn't even notice 'messy' Jesse's flaw! If she does, I may be in for big trouble, down the road.

CHAPTER II

Whining!

Most men are babies. They like to whine. When my hubby whines, I run the other way and go a search'n. The Yiddish word for whine is *kvetch*. I wrote this poem upon hearing Joe and our verbose friend, John Cantrell, *kvetch* one too many times. Maybe I'll nickname John Cantrell, John 'Kvetchrell,' if he doesn't quit 'kvetch'n.'

There are lots of men
Who kvetch all day
And when they do
I run away.

When e'er I hear
A grown man whine
Then I am so glad
That he is not mine!

But it is Joe's whining
That I often do hear.
But I can't run too far.
He's my hubby dear.

CHAPTER II

Enragement

When I get angry at my husband for not helping me in my search, or for other mundane reasons, I try to remind myself what he has to put up with at 56 years of age — four teenage daughters and a wife who, besides being quite a mess around the office and the home, has entered menopausal madness, as well.

To add insult to injury, Joe has a 10-year-old dynamo of a boy who is his Daddy's clone. Calling him his "110% boy," (i.e., whenever Joseph is around his Dad, it requires 110% of his energy to appease little Joe's irrepressible need for attention), it's like 'Dad spit son out.' Not to mention, our eldest brilliant son, who outsmarts his Dad in nearly everything except backyard basketball.

Whew! What a suffering hero my husband is... Or, could it be, he's a false martyr?

Maybe Joe is reaping the *karma* of something awful from out of his past. What

CHAPTER II

he's got, I'm sure he deserves. What on earth could he have done to merit such challenging conditions? He bears a heavy, heavy load.

I hope to learn to squelch my unholy rage at Joe's often compulsive behavior, knowing that his enormous task is virtually impossible — even though he may be getting what he deserves! Thanks for the grace of God, for without it, there's no way, José!

Is this what Joe deserves,
A madhouse all around?
Or is he just the hero
I have gladly found?

I've never met another
Who'd put up with this mess;
It's a marvelous sort of wonder.
Of this I do confess!

CHAPTER III

$\boxed{C}$ loset Skeleton

As I continue to search for the *Thingy*, I refuse to stand in line bored at a checkout counter. I'm just too impatient, or perhaps simply too utilitarian. I'm always searching to put my time to better use than stand idly by,

CHAPTER III

waiting for the sake of waiting. I want something to keep me occupied.

After waiting at the checkout counter and paying for our groceries, my hyper hubby (who spends his waiting time chatting with, or observing people), whispered, "Put that magazine down! Somebody's gonna arrest you for stealing words!"

Knowing that my charming, intelligent and beautiful Aunt Helen was (shut my mouth), a kleptomaniac, makes me feel quite sensitive to this genetic vulnerability. While in her 80's, Helen was picked up for hiding an item in her coat. Because of her age, the store manager simply gave her a lecture. "You should be ashamed of yourself, wearing a mink coat with a *can of tuna* hidden in it!" (I hope the Finklesteins don't get angry at me for exposing this closet skeleton.)

My clever Aunt was also an addict and expert at crashing exclusive parties in New York City. She knew the ropes and charmed her way in. At one of the parties, Marlon Brando accidentally spilled a drink on her

CHAPTER III

dress. He retorted, "Oh! I've christened your dress with my wine!"

When I visited Aunt Helen twenty-five years ago, she included me in her schemes, determined to find a millionaire man for me. Unfortunately, amongst the American elite in the Big Apple, I found nothing my heart was searching for, so I continued my look.

Helen was notorious for correcting everyone's improper use of the English language. A month before she died, I caught her for the first time in a grammatical error. I thought, "Uh huh, now's my chance to get back at her." So I corrected her and she replied, "I only use improper English on purpose."

Schwammi (my pet name for Aunt Helen) was born a beauty and insisted on staying that way, thus she became accustomed to face and body lifts after turning fifty.

This past summer, my notorious Aunt's time on earth was up and she went to meet her Maker. She had just recently turned 87. After an evening out with a friend, dinner, and going to the Broadway play, "Titanic," Helen passed

CHAPTER III

on — in her sleep. It wasn't like her to go anywhere without fanfare. She sort of snuck out, as it were, without warning — quite uncharacteristic of her! **Note: Aunt Helen was born during the years of the Titanic's construction, so her parting added an ironic and rather eerie footnote to a life lived in the fast lane.**

The Rabbi, who conducted Helen's funeral service, was expecting her to crash the event, knowing full well that Auntie loved to stir things up, to keep boredom in its place. The Rabbi's final words to us at the grave sight were, "May she rest in peace — or, whatever makes her most comfortable." He wasn't being unkind, just honest.

Aunt Helen's colorful, eldest daughter, an internationally acclaimed and celebrated writer, Gwen Davis, read her original poem which was written after learning of her mother's death. Helen had always encouraged Gwen, as a child, whenever she was feeling sad, to go and write a poem. So, Gwen wrote about her Mom crashing heaven, and meeting that 'Great Plastic Surgeon' in the sky, who will

CHAPTER III

forever keep her young and beautiful. Gwen's poem will be the basis for her next work. One of her previous books, **What A Way To Go** was made into a movie thirty years ago, starring Shirley MacLaine. *U-Can-Rent* that movie, just for the fun of it!

Awful Men!

I overheard my sister, Sorah, explain to my then 13-year-old daughter, Hannah Ruth, about how awful men are. Hannah retorted, "I know how awful men are... But I'm still going to marry one!"

Men are very awful.
We girls believe it's so.
Why do we want one to marry?
Don't ask me... I don't know!

Late one night in 1997, my sister demonstrated her skepticism of the male

CHAPTER III

population. At the time, she was staying in our Aunt Helen's vacant apartment at Central Park South in New York City.

Sister Sorah is as cute and pretty as can be for just entering her senior citizenship years. Thus, she devised a plan to camouflage herself as an *undesirable*. Transforming herself into a bag lady, she walked the streets unaccosted, and returned to Helen's apartment after taking in a late movie, outmaneuvering street rogues who often times lay in wait for vulnerable ladies such as herself.

Wearing a bright pink jacket with an old purple scarf, even beggars avoided her. Feeling an affinity with the homeless, Sorah played the role expertly and mumbled to herself as men and women of means walked briskly by her, peering right through her, as it were, with steely expressions and a sense of aloofness and self-preservation.

I should mention how my sister has been courageously battling cancer for many years. It must be her strong faith, a generous

CHAPTER III

sense of humor, and a bubbly spirit which also enables her to withstand the unpredictableness of the male species in particular, and of life in general. She's a *trooper!*

My Yankee transplant designer friend, Phyllis Zawislak, (Ms. Z) also has a love-hate relationship with those of the opposite sex. She has agreed to share with my readers about Adam's first questionable response about Eve, and why we ladies must continue to be on our guard. Hear ye Ms. Z — *Adam asked God, "Why did you make Eve so beautiful?" God answered, "So you would fall in love with her." Adam asked, "But why did you make her so stupid?" God answered, "So she would fall in love with you!"*

What goes around, comes around and, I suppose, coming down hard on the male species is not without its risks. So, beware, Ms. Z, who's entertained her fair share of negative male observations, became a victim of a freak accident while visiting family in Long Island, when a toothpick stuck in her big toe. It landed her in ER. Surviving the toothpick ordeal, and despite the pain, this freaky episode turned

CHAPTER III

into a laughing matter. Humor, after all, is the great balm for most any occasion.

Well, let me end this story before it becomes *'toe much ado about nothing!'*

atskills

In the Summer of '92, Sorah insisted that I and my three youngest attend Rosh Hashana (the Jewish New Year), at a retreat in the mountains called Chalet Vim. I didn't want to go, but I'm an easy mark for my older sister.

Since I do not drive, having been affirmed a hazard on the road, my girlfriend, Marti Buchanan, agreed to chauffeur us and let me backseat drive. I gathered my wits for finding the thingamajig, and we were soon zooming away to New York's Catskills for noshing (eating), spirited singing, and classes

CHAPTER III

taught by very learned Rabbis. Maybe they could give me a few clues in my search.

Marti sped ahead of the tropical storm, Danielle, that September day. We realized the seriousness of the storm as we were crossing the Chesapeake Bay Bridge, a 20-mile-long 'wonder of the world.' We **wonder**'ed if we would make it across the angry divide. The wild waves beneath made us seasick. Marti finally drove us to what we thought was safety, straight onto the New Jersey Turnpike. At this point, it was difficult to know which was worse, the traffic or the raging sea.

Next, on to the New York Thruway — or, was it? — We suddenly found ourselves on our merry way to New England! New York authorities never changed the signs that read New York Thruway. I suppose they wanted to hold passerbys at bay in New York State for as long as possible. I was more furious than Danielle's rage! I felt like suing that Yankee State for my extra travel time and additional toll fees. One New Yorker remarked to me, "All you'll get out of that is the inside of a bagel!"

In Search of the Thingamajig...

CHAPTER III

After Marti drove us out of the traffic maze, we were *amazed* to find Woodbridge. It was dark on the curvy mountain road, when an approaching vehicle abruptly sped by on our side. Marti quickly swerved the van to avoid a head-on, but there was no place to go except off a steep slope. "Oh Lord! Why aren't we rolling?" I thought.

We soberly climbed out of the teetering van. All four wheels were remarkably secured in the deep mud on the top of a rugged bank. It was cold and the kids were shaking. One cried, "I want to go home!" No cars were on the road, but soon a 'Good Samaritan' contacted a tow company. The tow man was shocked that the van didn't roll when we were in it, or as he towed it out. All acknowledged the miracle, and the van ran perfectly — onward and upward to the chalet.

We arrived late at Chalet Vim, where I was promptly escorted to my sobbing sister, Sorah, who was sure we were dead. Having prayed for us to be found alive, she promised God that she would never boss me again. The next day she tried to tell me what classes to

CHAPTER III

attend. I told her I was happy we were alive, and that she could continue to be my **boss**!

The staff gave us all the royal treatment. Mr. Vim and his employees fed us our Shabbos (Sabbath) dinner at which we were serenaded with live Hebrew singing as we noshed. As Marti wiped a tear of joy from her tired eye, I knew we were safe and sound, at last. The next morning we were made to feel right at home when they served grits for breakfast (kosher, of course). Later, I pushed my luck and urged Mr. Vim to include 'kosher collards' on the menu. He wasn't impressed.

During the weekend, the Rabbis were too busy holding classes for me to bother them regarding my comprehensive search.

Our drive back to North Carolina was wonderfully boring. We spent one night with my brother, Mike, in his Ardmore home near Philadelphia. Years ago, he gave us an old Apple MacIntosh Plus computer which allowed my Hubby and me to eventually get into the publishing business, which has made it possible for you to get to know about me and my event-filled search for the thingamajig.

In Search of the Thingamajig...

CHAPTER IV

*M*ushroom Hunt

The Countess Marion and her fourth husband of 22 years, Tony Weichel, have been my friends and neighbors for seven years, for better or worse. I first met Marion when she

CHAPTER IV

was 'pillaging' through my yard for mushrooms — and no, she did not do her first three husbands in. The first beloved husband, the Count, died tragically at an early age from an unfortunate accident.

The second dear husband, Vice-President for Twentieth Century Fox Studios, passed away after enjoying eleven years of marital bliss and international travel, jetting regularly between LA, New York, Paris, and Rome. He passed away from an unfortunate illness.

As for Marion's third husband, she may have felt like mushroom poisoning him, but she divorced him, instead.

Meanwhile, Marion has kept her fourth and, hopefully, *grande finale* husband alive and *pouchy*, with gourmet fix'ns for twenty-three years and counting! Tony offers a mixture of the best qualities of each of her past husbands, with an impressive creative flair added to the arrangement at no additional charge.

CHAPTER IV

The Countess is a most caring lady, who has a reputation for being quite mushy and sentimental at times. She is a Master Mycologist (mushroom expert) with many more credentials up her sleeves. There could be many volumes written about her, but I have not the space or time. I will give you a glimpse into her exotic life, beginning with her passion for specimens of the fungi type.

Marion's Marvelous Mushrooms

Some folks just crush mushrooms.
They don't even care
That mushrooms are so wonderful
To appreciate... So rare.

Some make homes for snails and ants.
They can grow on stumps, near plants.
Where nothing else would ever grow
There are mushrooms in a row.

Mushrooms can be for your health;
Some may even bring great wealth.
Some are poison, do not touch
Because your family loves you much!

CHAPTER IV

The Countess loves her mushrooms.
There are many kinds.
She hunts all over God's green earth
Until mushrooms she finds.

All shapes and sizes, colors neat,
Luscious, gourmet ones, to eat.
With joy our hearts do leap and leap.
Her recipes are such a treat!

P.S. You may purchase Marion's original recipes at her web site, www.delish.com. Hopefully, her husband will have it set up before this book becomes a best seller.

What's Countess Wearing

What is *Marion Frances Griswold de Cabrera Malo Camargo, La Condessa de Las Mercedes y Leonard y Weichel* wearing?

Since the Countess has clothes from all over the world, I caught myself searching for that 'Pied Thingamajig' in the inner chambers

CHAPTER IV

of her vast wardrobe. But, unfortunately, I found not the slightest clue within; although, I'm still a bit curious if it might, yet, be lurking someplace in there.

However, as for the Countess, she could care less about Vanna White's 'wardrobe of the day.' Fashion's no big deal to the Countess, having owned and worn only the most exquisite of fashionable garb most of her adult life. She cannot understand why everyone makes such a fuss over Vanna, exclaiming, "She would be so much better off if she simply wore one of my kaftans or galabeyas!" Actually, Marion seems to think Vanna's taste has improved a lot in '98.

"Folks hold their breath at social gatherings until the Countess arrives, anxious to view her attire," offered friend, Alameda Edwards.

At times her fashion statement is shocking. She can look as conservative as Nancy Reagan, but watch out for those occasions when she looks rather scandalous, intruding into Cher's fashion domain!

CHAPTER IV

Wheel of Marion

Sometimes she'll dress like Nancy,
But then she'll dress like Cher.
She always looks flamboyant,
I think it is a dare.
She has our rapt attention,
Living life on center stage.
At times she tries to shock us.
She'll always be the rage!

Punch'n Publisher

"Dine with the Countess at your own risk," my husband concluded after being jokingly slap/punched in the mouth at Charlie Tom's Restaurant. "The punch would not have hurt so badly if the Countess hadn't been bedecked in that enormous Egyptian five carat stone on her ring finger," exclaimed Joe. "Not only did she hit my lip, but she pulled and made fun of my aspiring new beard!" He added, "She can be dangerous!"

In Search of the Thingamajig...

CHAPTER IV

Marion's husband, Tony, saved Joe on this occasion by telling his gregarious wife to stop the abuse, even though Tony spends half of his time being upset at Joe himself.

Keeping his distance, it took Joe a while to recover and forgive. Yet, all is well that ends well. Marion has humbly apologized for hurting her favorite scapegoat. Joe will be damaged **'goods'** around the Countess, I project, from now on. He presently sits across the table from Marion whenever dining out with her, but not beside her. "I might be dumb, but I'm not stupid!" says he. "Stupid is as stupid does."

CHAPTER IV

issing!

The Countess Marion and Tony were at a Red Cross Seminar held at the beach. I was hoping Marion would find a valuable lead for me regarding my search.

Marion would rather shop and drop than sit in a boring meeting. Thus, at 1 PM, she told Tony that she would be back by 4 PM.

It was 5:30 and Marion had not returned. Tony called the police. At 6 PM Marion returned to the room where she loudly heard, "Where #*#*#*#* have you been?"

The Countess replied, "Why didn't you check the parking lot? I had a headache and fell asleep in the car." She dropped <u>before</u> she shopped!

She fell fast asleep
In her very own car.
He should have checked.
She wasn't that far.

CHAPTER IV

But men will be men.
That's all I can say.
Maybe they'll learn,
To trust us one day.

Next time I do hope
That when she does drop,
It won't be before
She goes out to shop.

Tony's Time Table

In my unrelenting search for the *whatch-a-ma-call-it*, I inquired of Tony, the husband of the fair Countess, simply, "What time is it?" He then wrote this definitive science report about the subject. I present it so that you may get to know the mind of Tony — greater than mensa level IQ and all:

"For eons there has been an ambiguous understanding about specific time periods in

CHAPTER IV

relation to other such periods. After extensive research, unlimited testing and painstaking deliberation, a final conclusion to the question of specific time measurement relationships has been reached. The following is the result of my findings, starting with the smallest measurable time period, the *instant:*

One Instant = The smallest time period

Six Instants = One Jiffy

Twenty Jiffies = One Soon

Four Soons = One After

Six Afters = One Later

Three Laters = One Maybe*

*(Maybe is not really a time period relevant to the scope of this study, but you may draw your own conclusion ....maybe.)

And for readers from the north....
1.333,333 *Maybes* = One -Two Shakes."

CHAPTER V

Friends

Oldies

I was asked by a classy fun-loving lady friend of mine, Alameda Edwards, "Why are most of your friends older than you?"

I shared, "Because most of them are more enjoyable to *puttsy* around with. Younger folks are busy social climbing, or some of them are too lazy, like myself, to climb up that shaky ladder in the first place!"

CHAPTER V

Mature ladies are more fun to pal around with, and they have time to help me in my search for that elusive thingamajig. I discovered that truth with my mother-in-law and her friends after I cunningly *hooked* my husband.

I'd like the world to know
I puttsy with the best.
You can't find any better
North, East, South or West.

The Bible Belt is good enough
To find ladies that please
With good old-fashioned gaiety
Resorting not to sleaze.

eighbors

A rather *weighty* neighbor of ours, the late Virginia Gerrard, was a solid senior citizen, but no match for a huge trash can by her house. She complained, "It sucked me in. I fell down, head first, with my feet dangling up in the air!"

In Search of the Thingamajig...

CHAPTER V

Washington's former Mayor, and a neighbor, Mr. Richard Tripp told her, "I would have given anything to have seen you!" Mr. Tripp has seen many other wonders in his world travels as an officer of the U.S. Navy and the U.S. Foreign Service. He put in radio transmitters in Russia and Iran and left Iran at the same time as did the Shah. Mr. Tripp played and worked vigorously in India, Pakistan, Korea and Southeast Africa. He's seen it all, and paints beautifully in water colors, portraying scenes he has personally viewed.

After Mr. Tripp's first wife died, he married Evelyn, who became 'mom' to his five children. Each adored their new mom. Richard and Evelyn have 15 grandchildren and 6 great-grandkids and counting. Yet, none of them, worldwide experiences included, have produced even one hint of a lead for me in my ongoing search. You can easily see how difficult my assignment has become. But don't think I'll give up!

CHAPTER V

Dreaming

My gracious lady friend, the very senior of citizens, Norfleet Hodges, has four college degrees and is most qualified to help me in my search. She told me about the time her friend told her that she was in his dream. She did not force him to tell her what it was about, saying, "I can't make myself behave in someone else's dream!"

I may not behave in your dream.
It's not my fault, I say.
So keep your dream to yourself
And I'll keep mine, if I may!

Norfleet ultimately behaved herself in my dream. We were in the Methodist Church to which she belongs. We saw quarters all over the floor. She was doing a much better job at gathering them than was I, much to my frustration and dismay. I still have a feeling of 'loss,' not beating Norfleet to all those quarters!

CHAPTER V

When I woke up from my dream, I immediately called Norfleet to share it with her. She shockingly informed me that she had had the very same dream several weeks earlier, but couldn't remember who the person was that she was with. We were dumbfounded.

Norfleet told me that after she collected the coins, it dawned on her that they really belonged to the church, so she gave them back. I probably would have kept them all, thinking I had found my long-sought-after thingama-*jangles*. After all, coins do *jangle*, don't they?

For us to share the same dream was more flabbergasting than fiction. It was a first for both of us, like spotting your first double rainbow in the sky.

Norfleet recently accused me of tolerating her 'mental gymnastics' in order to exploit her frivolous side, whenever it pops up. She is quite a character, like a lot of my friends in Washington the Original.

CHAPTER V

ot My Stuff

Our 67-year-old friend, John Cantrell, swept Isabella Woolard off her feet. Soon after the wedding, I telephoned my congratulations to them. John suddenly broke from talking and asked me to hold on. I then heard him pleading with Isabella, "People need stuff! Oh no! Not my bottles!"

I gathered from John's anxiety that day that anything which looked suspiciously worn or useless was headed for the nearby trash dump!

Poor John. All of his lifelong treasures, out the door... destined for a cold, uncaring trash heap... to insure his new bride's idea of **'home sweet home.'** If he had married his old friend, Velma, an avowed pack-rat, she would not have treated his treasures like refuse. She always adhered to the old saw, "One man's junk is another man's treasures."

CHAPTER V

Besides, John's Isabella could be carelessly tossing away a priceless thingamajig from amongst his things. Here's a nifty little ditty from poor John's perspective:

*Ya knew I was a pack rat.
Why did ya fall for me so?
I can't stand to have my treasures
Tossed in the dumpster, ya know!*

The Countess could not leave well enough alone when she heard about John's marital crisis. Thus she got inspired to write another ditty about poor John, and announces that it is to be sung to the music from Oklahoma's Poor Jud:

*John's things are gone.
Poor John's things are gone
And never will our John be the same;
John's things, they are gone
But a wife he has won
So don't have too much woe
For poor John.*

CHAPTER V

elma

     My dearly beloved 96-years-young and always-beautiful friend, Mrs. Zelma Winfield, was a successful Realtor. I asked her if she would appraise and sell my house. She graciously agreed and wanted 10% of the profits. Realtors usually only get 6% for homes, but she knew that I would be hard pressed to find a Realtor to list my house, so she played hard ball with me and charged 10% commission. What was I to do? She is my good friend.

     Zelma, ever the business lady, exclaimed, "It is a beautiful home and it would be worth $200,000, if a person could only live in it!" The house is a Victorian mansion but, unfortunately, it is only suitable for dolls. I had recently purchased it at the annual A-Z Doll Club Show.

     Mrs. Winfield thought she could sell it in the gift section of Carolyn's Fashions in Chocowinity, that she co-owns with Carolyn. Wonder if I'll find the thingamajig before she finds a buyer for my house.

CHAPTER V

Writers Bert and Naomi

My husband, Joe, recently told me, "When I grow up, I want to be just like Bert Brun." Bert's just ten years older than Joe and is writing an epic novel based on his European ancestry. His working title is "From Richer to Poorer."

Bert's lovely wife, Naomi Reed, recently published her own work, "Breakfast at the Prince of Wales." It is a success story about her and Bert's bed and breakfast inn located in Oregon. You may find it at your local book store or library.

When Naomi was coaxing Bert into dancing with her on a fund-raiser crossing of the Pamlico River on the Starlight Ferry Cruise, Bert said, "Most men really do not care to dance. They just use it as a way to get to the end of the evening!" Hmmm...? Will Bert's new book be provocative, or not?

CHAPTER V

Bert and Naomi have ridden their bicycles through several European countries. Who of us can say the same about themselves? I've, therefore, sought their assistance, and asked them to search their memory for any helpful information that would aid me in my search, realizing they've traveled widely and have seen so many amazing things.

Witchell Woes

Linda Witchell, another neighbor, who is a beach camping expert, was not a happy camper on this particular beach trip. It happened in their brand new tent. Linda's husband at the time, Jesse, woke her up at 2 AM, saying, "I need your help. I think we have a problem." He was lying on his big belly trying to unzip the entrance to the tent, because nature was calling him. He exclaimed, "It's stuck. It won't go up or down." At least the tent did not collapse on them like it did on another windy occasion. Linda is hoping

CHAPTER V

to write a book to memorialize their many camping mishaps.

Years ago, Linda was a professional Israeli folk dancer in New York. I asked her to start Washington's Israeli Folk Dance Troupe, made up of me and various non-Jewish friends. Our first performance was at the International Festival in Greenville, North Carolina. We were stupendous, if I must say so myself! Folks there couldn't believe that we came from this little town. It was great fun while it lasted.

But all good things must end, including this story, eventually this book, and, yes, my effort to find the you-know-what.

CHAPTER VI

*I*s it at Fu Sun?

It took the Countess, her husband, my husband and myself two hours of driving, one evening, to dine at Fu Sun Chinese Restaurant in Original Washington. Fu Sun is only one mile from our homes. It should not take more

CHAPTER VI

than four minutes to drive there, but that Saturday, my hubby, Joe, wanted to dine in Greenville, which is eighteen miles away with gobs of crowded restaurants — particularly, on weekends. This adventure was against my better judgment, but I surrendered to his will. Sometimes, I'm a real Saint — for short periods of time, anyway.

After checking out seven crowded restaurants in Greenville, Joe settled for the long line at Ragazzi's. I began pleading with him to return to our hometown, where we always get quick service at Fu Sun. I hate standing in line like cattle, but Joe insisted. Then I resorted to pitching one of my patented, Aunt **'Hellenic'** fits in front of the hungry folks who were patiently awaiting their turn at a Ragazzi's table.

Humiliated, my group split the scene, and I followed. They each severely chastened me on our way back to Fu Sun. But I knew best!

I do admire a woman who can behave like a lady in all circumstances. I hope that I

CHAPTER VI

do, in most cases, but the exceptions are what folks remember. I suspect this night won't soon be forgotten.

Once at Fu Sun, Dong, the delighted owner, treated us like the honored guests we often think ourselves. We sat down, alas, to a meal of fine Oriental cuisine — and, happily, no waiting in line before being seated.

A Jewish Princess I think I am.
And if I don't get my way,
Especially if I think I'm right,
I'll pitch a fit, I say.

My friends who accompany me
Are shocked, to say the least.
They never dreamed that I
Could behave like such a beast!

CHAPTER VI

Quazieball

The newest athletic game goes by the name Quazieball, and is patented as a variation of basketball for 'every person,' — except me, perhaps! Its inventor, Bill Booth of Original Washington. says, "The game incorporates elements of basketball, team handball, and chess and is designed to de-emphasize some athletic skills which largely depend on one's size and physical ability, while providing an opportunity for a greater number of participants than other mainline sports."

"Quazieball," says Bill, "will put an end to **'armchair'** basketball, and use half the space that is normally used for basketball. I plan the very first game and tournament to be held in Washington the Original."

I do believe that the Quazieball CEO thinks he has truly found what I've been searching for high and low. I'll have to see it played before I can say.

CHAPTER VI

Original Washington is definitely a place where unconventional ideas are born and bred and sometimes, even, where my outrageous and zany ideas stay alive and prosper.

Dong Ho

Quite by accident we discovered that all the employees at Fu Sun Restaurant are named Dong. This poem was written to honor our oriental friends, the Dongs, at Fu Sun.

To Fu Sun come along
Chinese food make you strong
Remember this song
They all are named Dong

Not a Sue, Kung or Ling
Let me ask you one thing
When you ring for Chow Ming
Couldn't just one name be Ding?

In Search of the Thingamajig...

CHAPTER VI

Gangsters

The founder and leader of Polly's Gang is none other than Polly Taylor, an ordained minister, who has a keen eye for fun. I suspect even the funerals at which she eulogizes become a bit more adventurous.

Jolly Polly is presently the Assistant Minister of Washington's First United Methodist Church, where she has recruited her gang members. One of Polly's projects is to hold a 'Fondue Revival' for her single gang members. Chocolate Fondue will be the principle fare.

Polly's Gang skips town quite a bit. When a famous political family was vacationing in Martha's Vineyard, Polly shared, "We're waiting for the unsavory element to leave Martha's Vineyard before I and my gang go!"

I tried to organize friends in my neighborhood to form *The Market Street Gang,* but it never jelled. I'd just like it to be a *wing* of Polly's Gang.

CHAPTER VI

To join their gang you need no money,
Knives, or not a gun.
Polly's gang in Washington
Must only bring some fun!

No time for gossip in their gang.
For certainly it's true:
It's idle talk that hurts a lot,
Not something they should do.

Where e'er they go or what they say,
It's always such a treat.
To qualify be young at heart,
Silly, smart, and sweet.

A new cult?

I held the first ever Buttercup Festival to crown Mrs. Samuel Mordechai as Washington's official *Buttercup Queen.* She truly merited the honor, not because she is most attractive and queen-like, but, rather, because she has

CHAPTER VI

inherited from her mother the lineage to let her buttercups simply be, in all their glorious spring season splendor.

One year, town authorities ordered her to mow her 'weeds,' or else. Her subjects rallied behind her. A petition was devised by Betty Perez, an attractive Yankee transplant to the Blount's Creek area, not far from the center of the universe, Original Washington.

I invited the Republican Candidate for Beaufort County Sheriff, Redden Leggett, to speak at the '98 Festival. He promised the Buttercup members that if elected, he would correct the City's insensitive intervention policy, and that it would happen *nary* again. Soon after his pronouncement, I volunteered to manage Redding's campaign. I do believe that my efforts were in vain, since Mr. Leggett came up short in the election that we all felt he should have won. The Buttercup lobby has some serious organizing to do to become a force in politics. However, my days of *politicing* are over.

During the Buttercup celebration of Festival '97, Lugene Worth had everyone wave

CHAPTER VI

their hands, pretending to be flowers. Then, Ed Voliva exclaimed, "Everyone driving by is going to think this is a cult!"

"Great!" I replied. "This has become the Buttercup Queen Cult!"

On that same occasion, Maurice Cunningham, an Irish Catholic Priest, who fell in love and married a nun who was and is a nurse midwife who ministered in Africa, led everyone in his original song to honor the Queen and proclaim her greatness. Polly Taylor, designed the Buttercup Crown for the Queen. 'The String Sounds of the Pamlico,' led by their violin instructor, Michelle Guererro, played mightily for her majesty. Moments later, the 'Bea'-*u-tiful* Bea Seal Simmons read an original ditty:

> *I'm just a little buttercup,*
> *Waiting for Mr. Wonderful*
> *To come and pick me up.*

Bea, who was 79, soon after the festival, was swept off her feet by Mr. Wonderful, Harold Simmons. They soon married. Then the

CHAPTER VI

glamorous Kay Currie, in all her dramatic glory recited her awesome ditty which she penned:

Roses are red;
Violets are blue;
But they don't get around
Like the Buttercups do.

And, this is my own ditty to all of my friends who missed the festivities for various reasons:

For failing to honor
The Buttercup Queen,
You'll end up in line
At the guillotine.

Don't miss it again.
And that's a decree.
You must show respect
For Her Majesty.

CHAPTER VI

Turnage Tales

Washington's ancient Turnage Theater, home for decades for early 20th century vaudeville and movie presentations, is being renovated. While I was discussing the project with Zena Hodges, she recalled an incident there that happened with herself and her husband, Ralph, in days gone by.

"During a particularly suspenseful part of a movie at The Turnage Theater, some 'young-un' in the row behind us slapped a sticky wad of Juicy Fruit gum onto the hair of Ralph's almost bald head. Mad as fire, he had to cut off the little bit of hairs he had left to get the gum out."

There are still 'playful happenings' in the Turnage. Recently, two businesswomen, who refused to be identified, heard heavy footsteps on the floor above them, while they were inspecting the building. They suspected it was a homeless man and exited quickly,

CHAPTER VI

locking the door. They phoned the current owner, Whit Blackstone, in order to have him check it out. He got on the case and reported, "It's empty and there are no stairs to climb to the top floor!" Later, Whiting Toler shared the fact that a lonely film projectionist committed suicide there many years ago. Could, I wonder, the *Ghost of the Turnage Past* be looking for some hard-to-find thing, like I've been engaged in doing so unsuccessfully these past years?

After the theatrical presentation of *The Blessed Be* at St. Peter's Episcopal Church in Washington, many folks were conversing about the hidden images they were discovering in the floating clouds backdrop on the stage, which was painted by local artist, Ginni Nickel. Some thought they saw Moses' face, which was eerie since the late Cecil B.

CHAPTER VI

DeMille, silver screen producer of Moses and *The Ten Commandments,* had been a member of St. Peter's.

Other folks thought Jesus' face was apparent in the cloud scene.

For weeks after the play, people were still going to view the 'image phenomena' hidden within the celestial sky that Ginni entitled *Thou Art.* Some folks saw three majestic images in one. Whenever anyone discovered one of the images, they'd gasp in amazement. One man found a lamb that others then saw; another, a heavenly horse; and another, an angel. Ginni's clouds were truly a surrealistic sight, filled with images galore for the imagination of most any observer.

Much to my dismay, the painting was soon removed from the church stage, shortchanging its public viewing. I felt I had missed another good opportunity. What could have been a discovery of the real 'McCoy,' ending my exhaustive search, proved, once again, that I was still in 'limbo land' of finding the thingamajig. I had to keep pressing on.

CHAPTER VI

plitt'n'

The Countess was waiting in line for a simple ice cream cone at Pamlico Provisions General Store in Washington. She watched in shock as artist, Ginni Nickel, designed her first banana split for a customer. Ginni is most talented and an occasional helper to her friend, owner 'Jimbo' McKeon.

The Countess shared with me about her experience, and of course, in her most inimitable manner: "Ginni is just *too* intelligent. She's certainly no *soda* jerk. I thought it was the most *ridiculous* banana split I ever saw, but of course, I didn't tell *her* that!"

Then Ginni, who has her *own* distinctive mannerisms told me a thing or two: "I was very nervous with the Countess standing in line, watching!" Ginni then described her creation: "It just developed into a mountain of cream, fruit and fluffy cloud-like stuff until it expanded beyond the bowl. It was actually

CHAPTER VI

splendid, I thought, not like Martha Stewart, you understand, but, rather, more like Julia Child whom, I think, would have approved of my creation and have placed a serving plate under the banana boat for it to float upon. It was a rather wonderful expression, if I do say so!"

I'm sorry I didn't see it. It may have ended my search.

Bon appetit!

The Countess watched Ginni
Make a banana split.
Piling it on and on,
It was too much to fit.

A 'fantasmagorical' creation
A sight to behold.
If it tasted a little funny,
At least it was cold!

In Search of the Thingamajig...

CHAPTER VII

Puttsying on the Pamlico

F erry Cruises

Judith Wycoff, owner of the Duck Blind Bed & Breakfast in Belhaven, became a single parent with the death of her first husband. She worked her way through college, law school, and became an attorney for the World Court, where she had the opportunity to meet the last

CHAPTER VII

surviving sitting judge for the Nuremberg trials. She also worked on the case of the PanAm Terrorist Bombing over Lockerbee, Scotland. Judith studied at cooking schools throughout Europe and Asia, including the famous **Cordon Bleu School** in Paris, France. Though she has traveled the world over, she reports to have had more fun on the Starlight Ferry Cruise on the Pamlico River between Bayview Shores and Aurora, than probably anywhere in her extensive travels. Judith was accompanied by her last, but not least, husband.

Alameda Edwards is an attractive lady who reeks with class, and is a *genuine* jetsetter, made so since her late husband worked as an airline pilot. She has jetted around the world many a time, but the ferry cruises over the Pamlico, she says, struck her fancy as much as anything she's experienced.

Lewis Forrest, a restaurant manager, consultant, and President of the Mattamaskeet Foundation of Hyde County, originally shared with me his brainstorm for having ferry cruise crossings of the Pamlico: "Arrange to have a

CHAPTER VII

live band play on board," he advised, "and invite folks to have a fun-time cruise." The idea stuck and the details were soon worked out.

After discussing the idea of music and festivity over the Pamlico with 'Head Honcho' for ferryboat regulations, John Gignilliat, our initial Starlight Cruise was up and running in short order. Van Respass entertained us with his accordion while we waited to walk aboard the '**N. C. Sea Level.**' Once on deck, we chatted, picnicked, and danced to the swing sounds of **'The Music Makers,'** a swing ensemble comprised of the singing mother and daughter duo of Lil Etchison (guitar), and Jennifer Murdock (drums). Lugene Worth organized the daring, in line dancing and interpretive dances.

We began our journey over the reflective waters of the Pamlico with a southerly breeze blowing gently across our bow. To the delight of curious eyes and ready ears, our vessel was escorted by laughing gulls, squawking and dutifully attentive as they glided swiftly back and forth from stern to bow and port to starboard. Their fluid and rhythmic uniformity

CHAPTER VII

was a sight to behold. A spectacular setting fireball blazed against a cloudless western sky, as we maneuvered into our river course.

Following the music, picnicking, and socializing on the far side of the river, the *Sea Level* reversed course and ferried a path away from its Aurora port. Returning upon its watery highway, which was now darkened by nightfall, yet now reflecting the night sky's greater and lesser lights, an equally spectacular scene presented itself — a sort of double feature, if you will. Every eye and every heart was captivated, as evening stars splashed and dashed, glistened and twinkled against the outer edges of the moon's brilliant glow. The romantic nuance of a full-blown Carolina moon bathed its subjects in southern delight — in a style you'd have to see and feel, for yourself, to fully appreciate.

Indeed, it was a full-blown and surreal evening-scape, one that seared minds and melded hearts into a shared oneness. Only advancing years of one's dotage would put closure to the vividness of this magnificent cruise! The conjunction of such sights, sounds,

In Search of the Thingamajig...

CHAPTER VII

and experiences capped what, best, could be described as a 'trip to heaven and back.'

But, did I discover the thingamajig across the Pamlico that evening? No. Not, unless, you count a 'taste of heaven' as a qualifier. Yet, that's exactly what we enjoyed, on this, our inaugural ferryboat cruise. But, don't fret, I'm ever watchful and on-the-ready to find my heart's thingamajig-throb. I did find 'peace of mind' over the waters of the Pamlico.

On another Pamlico crossing, we enjoyed a masquerade cruise. It was most creative. I dressed as 'The Pied Piperess,' and played my pipe while leading the courageously costumed cruisers onto what I announced as the 'Mini Titanic' — just to add a bit of spice and drama to our excursion.

It was a bit nippy on that occasion, and I was ever so thankful when one *cruiser* lady warmed us all by disguising herself as 'The Sun.' She was awarded first prize for best outfit. The prize was a cake, 'yummily' created by Cathy Smith, and readily consumed by envious cruise guests, guilt-ridden as many of them were.

CHAPTER VII

I, the Judge, must admit that my judgement was, how shall I confess, *'rigged.'* I knew Mrs. Sun would be willing to share her booty with the masqueraders, even before the prize was awarded. Mrs. Sun ultimately revealed herself to be, whom else, but the spunky and theatrical Marti Buchanan.

The stickiest calamity occurring during our cruises was the event when Catrita Andrews found herself knee deep in the salsa. Exclaimed Catrita, "I have no idea how it happened. I was scurrying to put out refreshments, when that big bowl of salsa came tumbling on down all by itself." No one had the gumption to own up to the mess, however.

The most frightful time experienced on any of our cruises happened to my fellow 'scavenger,' Susan Pickens. Susan, who is a super ICR nurse, brought her son Michael (who reminds me of the cartoon character, Bobby, in 'Bobby's World'). It wasn't enough that Michael hung from the bars on the upper deck of the ferryboat, scaring his mother half to death, but, while docked on the other side of the river, young Michael 'abandoned ship' for

In Search of the Thingamajig...

CHAPTER VII

the adventure of seeking sharks teeth in an area which included the nearby snake-infested grasses adjacent the ferryboat landing site. His appetite had been whetted months before, in collecting old fossils, when my husband had taken him to what is known in nearby Pinetown as 'Shark Tooth Mountain.'

Michael just may be the one I need to enlist in my own search. He's fearless and curious. What more would a thingamajig-seeker need? I should talk to Susan about this...

I mustn't forget fellow cruiser, Dawn Cahoon, in my litany of interesting ferryboat guests. Dawn is from Swan Quarter, a quaint, out of the way village by the edge of the Pamlico Sound. She is well traveled and, for five years, lived on beautiful Guam, half way around the world. Having partaken, herself, she now boasts to others of our fabulous ferry cruises. Dawn's looks reminds me of the Mona Lisa.

Another fascinating cruise guest is Ernest Stevenson, the country's first Afro-American Navy Seal member, and, more

CHAPTER VII

recently, an active Washington Boys and Girls Club Board Member. Ernest worked on the **'United States Steamship Lake Champlain,'** recovery ship and aircraft carrier. After that, he was in the United States Marshal Service, working with the Black Muslim trials. He was Gorden G. Liddy's escort to trial and guardian of the Watergate tapes. He's had many notable experiences, including converting to Judaism, but cruising the Pamlico under a full moon on a balmy evening is a treat he, too, relishes with the rest of us.

Theme cruises (such as a Murder Mystery 'Who-Done-It' Cruise) keep the ferryboat crews 'hopping,' and prospective cruise guests 'hoping' for another fun adventure. I haven't found the thingamajig on any of my many crossings of the Pamlico, thus far, but I've found that 'Special Something.'

Come join us on the ferry,
Where everyone is merry.

If on the cruise you just chat,
You shant lose your fat.

So dance and do not be dreary!

CHAPTER VII

Chef's Blend

Ron and Jamie Peabody, 'Hot'lanta' transplants, are a young couple that are not crabby and have much creative zeal and energy. They are smart and business-minded enough to be coconspirators with me in my search.

Ron is marketing Culinary Crustaceans, the Chef's Blend's line of condensed seafood bases. It is the culmination of 15 years of fresh crab and seafood production experience.

Speaking of crabs... Belhaven on Pungo Creek (a tributary of the Pamlico River), is the site of an annual crab festival. At one such event, a portrait of **'yours truly'** was hung on the wall at Eeii's Little Corners of the World Art Gallery. Painted by my 'out-of-the-closet' secret admirer, it created a stir opening night, since my hair was painted bright purple even before colored hair became a Dennis Rodman fashion statement.

CHAPTER VII

Artist and co-owner, Effie Ray Goff (her other half is Julian), lamented, "That purple hair! I didn't even know what painting to hang next to it. It would have to be something strong!"

Ain'cha Glad?

The Peabodys (my aforementioned coconspirators) and I are tenaciously sticking to the effort to discover the whereabouts of the *you-know-what*. In my search, I carefully listen for one-liners and succinct sound bites that capture my imagination and that, I think, of my fans, as well. Here's an example I heard recently:

Buzz Cayton was sitting on the lawn next to his wife, Chris, who was sitting next to me, at the Pamlico Waterfront Dixieland Band Concert. Suddenly Buzz exclaimed, "Oh no! A bird just christened my shirt." In a quick afterthought, he added, "I'm sure glad cows don't fly!"

CHAPTER VII

We can thank the dear Lord
That cows do not fly.
After Buzz's experience
I needn't tell you why.

If nuts fall on your head
When you're under a tree
Ain'cha glad watermelons
Can ne'er fall on thee?

Redden Leggett was campaigning to be our next Beaufort County Sheriff. Much to my dismay, he agreed to let me be his Campaign Manager, and, to cut to the chase, he lost.

Redden is a massive 6'5" hunk of an African-American. He is also a conservative Republican entrepreneur and is a former SBI man who once had ownership in two McDonald's franchises in Philadelphia. He also

CHAPTER VII

made the last cut for the old Philadelphia Bullets Basketball Team in his younger years.

During the campaign for Sheriff, however, I invited him and his wife, Linda, on a Starlight Ferry Cruise. I announced to the cruisers that he was our 'body guard' for the evening, and they had better vote for him or else. Then Kay Currie, our moderator that night, invited him to the mike.

I thought, "Oh no! He's going to talk on and on and the swing band has only an hour to play. Thus, after a minute and at a point which sounded like a good ending, I began to lead an applause, moving toward the mike. I thanked him profusely, and he made his way to the upper deck. Some thought that it was rather brave of me, since I am only a petite lady.

My dear friend, Sadie Haislip, approached Redden, and in her thick Southern drawl, she asked him, "If you get to be our next Sheriff, are you going to let little ladies like that boss you around?"

He replied, "Only until I get elected!"

In Search of the Thingamajig...

CHAPTER VIII

Spanning the Globe

B urk-avarious

The Burke's arrived 15 miles from our home, in Old Bath Towne, on their sailboat, *Kitara*. Bath was a haven for the pirate, Blackbeard, and has became a regular haven for the Burke family, who have circumnavigated the world and crisscrossed the Atlantic seven times in 15 years with their two children and cats *numero one* and *two*, and no mice.

CHAPTER VIII

The father, Patrick, is from Ireland. A very gifted man, he built their sailboat *home*, crafts classical guitars, which he plays, and violins, which his son, Joshua, plays. Both record. Diana is the vivacious wife and mother, who is a poet/writer, originally from South Africa. Patrick and 13-year-old son, Joshua, perform together when-ere they're invited.

I dub Joshua's violin the 'Burke'avarius, after the grand quality of sound and construction of the famous Stradivarius.

Joshua played 'second fiddle,' for a while recently, as the youngest member of the **East Carolina Symphony** in nearby Greenville. Dr. Ara Gregorian, a graduate from Julliard, and now head of the string section at East Carolina University, is Joshua's teacher. Joshua has also 'concerto-ed' with my son Jesse at several performances.

Like her mom, 15-year-old Zoe Burke is a gifted writer and observer of life. At the risk of being politically incorrect to some of Irish descent, Zoe and my daughter, Hannah Ruth, were dubbed the 'freckle-sisters.' One day I

In Search of the Thingamajig...

CHAPTER VIII

heard Zoe exclaiming in her unique dialect, "I'm so afraid I'll catch the Southern accent." Then she accused her mother of giving her a 'mother' look. It's commonly known that Zoe 'turns nose up' at that 'New York' accent, as well.

Since the world is their 'country,' I am hoping to get some good leads for my *search* from the Burkes. They are such a delightful and creative family. You must count it a privilege if, per chance, you cross paths with them and the many talents their clan has to offer. I hope to hear, one day soon, that Mom and daughter Burke have written a book about their divers adventures.

The Burke's sail around the world.
Kitara is their cozy home.
And when they did arrive in Bath,
No longer did they care to roam.

They entertain all kinds of folks
In many a different land.
For them to spend their time with us
Is nothing less than grand.

CHAPTER VIII

Kenya's Khadija

Khadija of Kenya lived in our home for a month. I was hoping she, too, would be of help in my search. She is presently a nurse at the Pungo District Hospital in Belhaven, which is not far from the small town of Bath. Both towns remind Khadija of Kenya.

Khadija first left her homeland at age 35 with the blessing of her husband and two children to work for a Prince in Saudi Arabia for three years. She took care of the pregnant Princess and then her new baby boy.

Khadija shared, "At first, life was nice and full of fun. We traveled to Italy, France, Germany, America, Mexico, Indonesia, Singapore and Egypt, staying in the best hotels.

However, traveling with them got very crazy. Packing and unpacking. Every dress had matching shoes, handbag, and eyeglasses. They changed their clothes four times every

CHAPTER VIII

day. Exhausted, tempers would flare. The Princess often abused her workers, except for me, since I took care of the baby."

She related, "The Princess was supposed to be right all of the time and the Prince was like her puppet."

I said to Khadija, "The Princess must be beautiful!" She replied, "She was fat and ugly. The Prince was fat and ugly, too."

I was most curious to find out if Khadija had met the Princess' grandfather, King Fahd.

She said, "I once took the baby to him for a blessing. Because I could speak English, he thought I was the most learned person in the world."

I asked her what impression she had of the king. She exclaimed, "They are all ignorant, arrogant and cruel. They play with money like it is a toy and do not pay their workers for six months, or help them in any way. The baby was cute, though."

CHAPTER VIII

When I told Khadija that her adventure was going to be in my book, she exclaimed, "I hope the Prince won't come after me! Please don't translate it into Arabic."

Here's hoping that ol' Prince won't come after Khadija with a thingama-Arab.

Arapahoe

There is a little 'one-horse' community in Pamlico County up route 55 from New Bern and some 40 miles from Washington, called Arapahoe. I thought my search would end at their annual **Bethlehem Walk**.

Their unique Bethlehem Village springs to life every mid-December, with a hundred costumed actors, with whom folks may interact as they walk through the village of Jesus' day. It is recommended that travelers avoid beggars who crave your alms and merchants who haggle to buy lady travelers (if the prospect's feet are big enough to crush grapes).

CHAPTER VIII

Roman soldiers keep the peace as we meander through time.

Be ever so mindful if you traverse through this village, because the signs are all in Hebrew and you may get confused. So, don't fall into the water at the fishing village or get in the way of the Israeli dancers, and do beware of the rude innkeeper. Do not get too dismayed, however, because singing angels will soon appear from nowhere and guide you to the the straw-filled manger!

Grandfather Raven, the Chief Elder of the **Shoshawnee Indian Tribe,** is a friend of my sister, Sorah. They met at a health spa in Mexico, where he taught her a great deal of Native American history. He also wished to adopt her according to their custom.

CHAPTER VIII

Raven's mother was born into an Orthodox Jewish family. When she married an Indian Chief, her family sat shiva for her. This means that they mourned for a week for her as if she were dead. Then, she moved to the Indian Reservation and had 'three little Indians.'

After all of this, Raven's father abandoned his wife and children and the life they led on the reservation, in order to go to Hollywood and act in cowboy and indian movies. Raven's Mom tried to leave the reservation with her three children, but the elders made her leave one behind. It was Grandfather Raven, who is now 77. His mother is still alive at 107. (Mazel Tov!)

My sister has taught Grandfather Raven about our Jewish Tradition. I hope he found the thingama-pow-wow for all his effort!

In Search of the Thingamajig...

CHAPTER IX

Captured Hero

Mr. Lai Nguyen, a South Vietnamese aerial photographer during the Vietnam War, was shot down six times and finally captured. Lai spent a month in our town, sponsored by St. Peter's Episcopal Church, before being reunited with relatives in Houston, Texas. During his stay, he photographed many folks at gatherings to show his gratitude.

CHAPTER IX

Lai and his daughter attended an Hawaiian concert at my home, which included singer, Malcolm Makua and dancer, Lugene Worth. (Lugene was a professional dancer and also Lucille Ball's and Jill St. John's personal trainer a few decades ago. Now she shares her many talents for the folks in our area.)

The yam was the focus of my food reception. I served yam-laced cookies, dip, chips and **'chews.'** Lai informed me, "All I ate was yams the six years I was in prison!"

I replied, "Oh no! I 'yam' very sorry!"

Captain Hill

I never cease to be amazed about the background of some of my Washington friends. Captain John Hill is one of them. He is not just your normal run-of-the-mill Naval Captain. He is the son of Vice Admiral Hill, the Commander of the **Amphibious Assault Forces,** which captured the islands of Siapan,

CHAPTER IX

Tinnian, Guam, Tarawa, and Iwo Jima from the Japanese during World War II. He took the surrender of the Japanese Forces in southern Japan, while General MacArthur accepted the surrender of the northern forces.

Due to Captain John's Dad's heroism, John was recently invited to ride on the **U.S.S. Harry W. Hill** (DD986) for its last sea venture on its return home from the Persian Gulf 33 years after Captain Hill's last command. I begged him to be on the lookout for the thingamajig on this last voyage, but he returned with *nary* a discovery.

He won WWII

During one of my intensive thingamajig searches, I learned that when Jake Zwaal, a colorful Dutch Immigrant friend of mine, was a teenager in Holland, he was the reason the Allies won World War II — to hear him explain it.

CHAPTER IX

The story began when the Nazis were in control of Jake's homeland. Having met a young Nazi soldier, Jake challenged him to a chess match. Jake said to him, "If I win, then the Allies are going to win the war. If you win, then the Nazis will win the war." Jake played his heart out.

In his adorable Dutch accent, Jake explained to me, "I played like heck! The black figures were the Nazis. I played the white. Luckily, the soldier was a good sport when I won the game!"

Jake lives in the nearby countryside of Terra Ceia, where he is a real 'hit' at the colorful **Dutch Tulip Festival** presented there, annually. Playing the harmonica, bicycling, nutrition and dancing keeps this charismatic Dutch 'dude' in shape.

A better friend no one does make
Than this musician we all call Jake
He dances 'til the floor does shake
And does it all 'for goodness sake.'

CHAPTER IX

Rude Bernadette!

Does Bernadette hold the key to my quest to find the watch-a-ma-call-it? I doubt it. Let me tell you why. First of all, she is a rather peculiar spinster of a teacher from France who chaperones exchange students to the United States during the Summer.

My special neighbors, the Voisards, were assigned to be Bernadette's host family. Pierre Voisard was thrilled at the opportunity to brush up on his French. He was born in Quebec. Upon arriving at her host family's home, Bernadette announced to Pierre and his wife, Jenay, that she was in America to speak English only! Then she said, "I'm not here to help you, or clean my room. I'm on holiday," said she.

Soon after, Bernadette demanded that Jenay immediately remedy the food situation explaining, "I'm on a health food diet."

CHAPTER IX

Bernadette needed help each time she operated an electronic device. She turned the light knob the wrong way until it screwed out, and then announced it was broken. After a week of lessons, she mastered the door locks. The Voisards were going to take a picture of the door in a locked position for her to use as a reference.

Before lending her their car, they tested her skills. She changed lanes without looking, telling them, "In France, drivers get out of the way!" When stuck behind traffic, she put both feet hard on the brake pedal, and gave Pierre a wild look, saying, "The car is broke. It won't move!"

When Bernadette walked just two blocks from the Voisard home, she got lost and became hysterical, until a 'Good Samaritan' came along and escorted her back from whence she came.

Bernadette was terrified of Pierre's large parrots, one of which escaped his cage to join her at breakfast. After tasting and disliking her yogurt, the parrot tossed Bernadette's tray to the floor. She ran screaming to her hosts.

CHAPTER IX

The Voisards learned that Bernadette's French students were forced to take charge at Chicago's airport in what became the 'Second French Revolution.' She had become so disoriented and out of control in the terminal that her students had to *usher* her to their plane.

After three weeks of trials and tribulations, the Voisards reached the end of their rope and asked Bernadette to leave. I offered to take her into our home even though she once scolded my husband, "Shut up. You talk too loud!"

I actually communicated with her well enough and began probing about the thingama-wee-wees in France. But, she was not the least bit interested in staying in our messy mansion, even though she knew she had worn out her welcome at the Voisards.

Then my friend, Sadie Haislip, felt sorry for Bernadette after she complained to her about how terrible her treatment was at the Voisards. Sadie never met that 'mean' couple and was compelled to rescue Bernadette by

CHAPTER IX

being the perfect hostess. After one week, Sadie exclaimed to me, "I always invite my guests back except for this most self-centered one! The only thing she liked about our country was the ice water served in the restaurants!"

After Bernadette realized she forgot her ticket while boarding her plane to Paris, Sadie's neighbor, who drove Bernadette to the airport, wanted to buy her a new ticket rather than chance her staying in the country any longer!

We'll never forget
'Darlin' Bernadette
Who must have her way
Or else we would pay!

She was on exchange
And acted quite strange;
But I didn't mind
To her I was kind.

Her rudeness did show
But I still liked her so;
I hope she'll see not
The fame she's now got!

CHAPTER IX

The French were redeemed in the eyes of the Voisards, after hosting an exceptional Frenchman, who displays the epitome of charm. Docteur Christian Pheline, of Orleans, is a retired Neurosurgeon and a fine artist.

The Docteur was invited to my home for dinner one evening, but upon his arrival, I was still bathing. For beautiful skin, my bath consisted of salt and a teaspoon of spirit of turpentine. Finished, I entered his presence, and he exclaimed, "Mademoiselle, you smell just like a painting!" I wish that I could share with my readers all of the many 'sweet nothings' that the Docteur expressed to me, but they are conveniently lost in my memory bank.

All of my lady friends flipped head over heels over the Docteur, including the Countess. The Docteur even offered to have an art class in my friend Phyllis Carver's home. He could have charmed the you-know-what off of any you-know-what. However, unlike the antics of the now infamous Bernadette, he was the perfect gentleman and will be welcomed back when the time comes!

CHAPTER X

General Hospital

UFO?

When none of my home remedies worked, my husband, Joe, asked several pharmacists in town to peer down his throat. They were all perplexed at the strange growth protruding from the gum's surface. Joe knew then that he must find Dr. Young. Richard Young, M.D., a very popular doctor in our

CHAPTER X

area, is the spitting image of the *George* character in the 'Seinfeld' series, with every bit as much spark to his personality. However, to his wife, Judy, a dental hygienist, he reminds her of Jack Benny, and I agree. He is quite theatrical, having starred in some of the local Washington Community Theater Association plays. Thus, for all his talent, I trusted that Dr. Young would help to solve Joe's troublesome problem.

When my husband found the good doc, he exclaimed, "Hmmm. I have never seen anything like that!" He then referred Joe to Greenville's ENT (eyes, nose and throat specialist), William Bost.

Like most men, Joe can be a real baby about medical matters. I called all my friends to pray about the problem. It looked serious. It was no laughing matter.

During Joe's initial visit, Dr. Bost and his assistant, Brenda Gray, immediately yanked the 'growth' out, as brave Joe gagged.

CHAPTER X

Relieved, Joe was elated that it came out without too much ado. The three observed this 'unidentifiable foreign object' (UFO).

Dr. Bost exclaimed, "It does resemble a meteorite cinder, or something from outer space. Maybe, a petrified UFO relic of some sort. I've just never seen anything like it on this earth."

Joe interjected, "It looks like a shriveled, *mummified* wisdom tooth, to me!"

The next day, the Countess Marion said, "Joe had better not sleep with his mouth open, anymore!"

Well, my 'Joe-ffeur' has a new lease on life, now that his throat has healed. He sighed, "I feel like I dodged a bullet with my name on it!" Thank goodness, he can still assist me in my search.

CHAPTER X

Dentist

When The Countess Marion walked into her 15th Street dentist's office, her dentist, who refuses identification, inquired, "Are you really a Countess? I've been reading about you."

She let him know that I am the 'big mouth' that made her famous by featuring her exploits in *The Pamlico Scoop Journal/Advertiser* — when I am not engrossed in my searching, that is.

When the dentist found out from the 'horse's mouth' that it is true, he apologized profusely for all the pain he had caused her.

After the Countess shared with me about their conversation, I ghost wrote this poem to the Countess from the dentist's point of view:

Begging Your Countess' Forgiveness

I beg for your forgiveness.
For causing so much pain.
Please take my apology
I'll use more novacaine.

CHAPTER X

Where've I been these many years?
Was my mind just a blur?
How foolish of me not to know
The Countess that you were.

Another dentist may be worse,
So with me you should stay.
I'll do my best to satisfy
And I'll not make you pay.

I'd really hate to lose you.
I'm honored to have you here.
I'll be so very gentle.
There's nothing more to fear.

I also hear you travel far,
To Turkey, France and Spain.
I'll gladly be your chaperone.
Great knowledge will I gain.

I can't believe you're so well read,
The classics, great and small.
Your husband can just take a walk.
Your charm doth make me fall!

In Search of the Thingamajig...

CHAPTER X

Cry Baby

Lovie Shelton, a pioneer Nurse Midwife, has heard more cries than anyone I know. She trained at the **Edinburg School of Midwifery** in Scotland and returned to North Carolina to await the arrival of many new earthlings. In fact, she has been in 3,000 homes. Lovie's midwifery work is exhibited at the North Carolina Museum of History in Raleigh.

Having grown up on a farm, Lovie cares for animals, and loans out Gus, her special mule, to 'star' in Arapahoe's annual Bethlehem Walk production. She says, "He's elderly, you might say. Almost 30-years-old, but he does the job and looks the part." Her goats have also been part of the production. At the present time, Lovie hears a different cry. She is a Hospice Volunteer. However, I think she is still available for an occasional bambino, when pressed into action.

CHAPTER X

Back Cracker

Doctor Englehardt is a curmudgeon. His bark is worse than his bite. Down deep, he is one of the kindest men one could ever know. As a Chiropractor, he's more like the old-fashioned family doctor who discusses your health problems and daily nutritional requirements.

At 85, Doc is still practicing on folks and practices what he preaches. Every morning, he jumps on the trampoline and does 20 push-ups claiming, "I'll die with my boots on!"

Retirement is a dirty word to him. He's as spry as a fox and puts younger men, with their jelly bellies, to shame. Doc has danced with me on the ferry cruises, but he's too active to have the time to aid me in my search.

If you need a crack
Somewhere in your back,
Don't go to a quack.
Englehardt's not slack.

In Search of the Thingamajig...

CHAPTER XI

Scandalous Yesteryear

My husband's beautiful and artistic sister, Jayne Davis Wall, displayed an alleged provocative painting at the Beaufort County Arts Council Show, causing an eruption of gossip. My dear husband was the culprit.

The impressionistic work exhibited two

CHAPTER XI

women posing together in wedding gowns. My Joe, who definitely has the 'gift of gab,' not necessarily the 'gift of social discernment,' volunteered an 'interpretation' of the painting to his friend and fellow roommate back in their single days, Larry Windley. He promoted to Larry that Jayne's scene depicted a same-sex marriage, never expecting it to go any further than amongst the folks who were admiring the vibrant colors for which Jayne's paintings are celebrated. However, things didn't stop there. Indeed, not!

Scandal is not new to my husband and his sister's ancestry. The branch of controversy doesn't fall far from the tree. Joe and Jayne's Nanny shocked the whole of 'little' Washington with her fling with the 'milkman' in 1921. Thus, their extremely honorable and beloved Granddaddy divorced her, back when divorce was as uncommon as infidelity to White House occupants has become common. It seems Granddaddy discovered love letters of the affair. (One source offered that the boyfriend was hiding in the closet when Granddad discovered him.)

In Search of the Thingamajig...

CHAPTER XI

Nanny was a beauty and an extra special fun-loving gal, and despite having a prominent and remarkable husband, she was rather lonely, since he was so involved in his work. Grandma disclaimed an actual physical involvement with 'the milkman,' but Gramps, despite loving her dearly, could not deal with such an indiscretion.

Grampa did what he must.
When she destroyed his trust.
Despite this defeat,
She never did cheat.

That's what she said,
But since they're both dead,
We never will know,
If it really t'was so.

I shall delve no further but proceed to pamper myself at the Korner Beauty Shop and thence puttsy further down Main Street to purchase a violin at Carver's Music Center.

And yes... Joe's interpretation was just that... **His** interpretation! He should have bitten his tongue. The two ladies in Jayne's picture were not what Joe had said. So there!

CHAPTER XI

*L*uger Legend

Once upon a busy time, Joe and I were staying at the Pittsburgh Marriott at the same time as the famous professional wrestler, Lex Luger, the 280-lb behemoth and heir-apparent to the World Wrestling Federation Championship. However, he was no match for me, no thanks to my husband.

When I spied Lex in the hotel lobby, I approached him with my credentials for an interview. Lex said, "Sorry, this is the day I spend with my wife and children."

Then, I casually asked him, "If you don't want to draw attention to yourself, then why are you wearing such flashy cloths?" (He wore a tight-fitting stars and strips outfit.)

He exclaimed, "Lady, you are rude?"

I replied, "You are behaving just like those wrestlers on tv I see!"

CHAPTER XI

Getting madder by the second, he countered, "Look lady, I'm normally a nice guy, BUT..." Then my husband meandered onto the scene, taking a speedy seat on a nearby couch so as to camouflage his great size disadvantage.

"What's going on?" Joe, ever so softly, ventured.

Lex loudly responded, "This lady is being rude."

He grabbed his children and continued his tirade, "Let's get out of here!"

This scene is an example why my youngest daughter, Rebekah, known, herself, as the 'mouth of the South,' (to her own discredit), has dubbed her mom, 'The Embarrasser.'

The snack bar waitresses told us, shortly after our testy encounter, "Lex was quite pleasant with us."

I may have missed my calling as a lady wrestler! My personality just might work.

CHAPTER XI

L ost Colony?

Playwright Paul Green's **The Lost Colony,** playing in Manteo, North Carolina, is one of the nation's most colorful and longest-running outdoor dramas. Thus, I figured that I may at least get some leads in my search for the thingamajig from the cast and crew at the season's opening night reception. I arrived with a Pamlico Scoop press pass and was soon chatting with the House Manager, Bob Kretz. As he filled his plate, two meatballs bounced to the floor. Bob, ever so discreetly, surveyed the guests and gently kicked them under the banquet table!

I continued gabbing with the 'meatball kicker,' as he attempted to defray attention elsewhere, exclaiming in disbelief, "I would not get any more meatballs if I were you! That old man just stuck his whole hand in them!" Soon after, I observed the new Public Relations Director consuming the unsanitary meatballs and proceeded to warn her of the problem. Then I informed her about the bouncing meatball mess which ended up under the table,

CHAPTER XI

and suggested playfully getting back at the culprit. "Complain to Bob," I offered, "that you found meatballs under the table that some sorry soul must have kicked there."

The ploy succeeded famously at poor Bob's expense, and we continued the evening without partaking of any more meatballs.

aked Truth

Whiting Toler, a born and bred Washington artist, shared with me: "I loved reading that story in The Scoop about the rude French guest." I told him that I neglected to write about the time Bernadette stormed into the Voisard's bedroom unannounced.

Pierre was stark naked, to which she exclaimed, "It bothers me **not** one bit!"

CHAPTER XI

Whiting then told me about his experience with the two French girls and a guy hitchhiking through America. He generously offered to take them to the ocean. On the way, however, while Whiting stopped for an errand, his riders got out of the car and changed into their bathing suits, right in the parking lot, before passing cars and pedestrians. Whiting returned a bit shocked, and pleaded with them, saying, "Stop waving back to the people honking their horns at you!"

If you have lunch in our town at The Meeting Place on Main Street, you will see Whiting's interesting art work. Alice Stallings, a very fine artist, herself, examined the art on the wall, explaining, "Whiting's paintings are a nostalgic look of old Washington, painted directly on the two walls. They are rather large scenic views."

Artist Ginni Nickell experienced the work and wrote... 'The light that is transmitted from that magnificent work is pure and radiant; emitting the vision of a true master!'

In Search of the Thingamajig...

CHAPTER XI

As one is eating at the Meeting Place in Downtown Washington, and admiring Whiting's work, an excellent classical guitarist, Smith St. James, entertains daily from noon until 3 PM. Smith escaped the madness of New York City life several years ago for the quietness of our town. Our town has become a haven for a virtual variety of artists of many ilks, and that's the 'naked truth!'

In the Bible Belt and Beyond

CHAPTER XII

Carolina Journal

The Maestro and Sam's Bull

Renowned concert pianist and composer from Paris, the late Daniel Ericourt performed for the Queen of England, at Carnegie Hall, and in forty nations around the

CHAPTER XII

world. He and his Washington-born and equally-talented wife, Jayne Winfield Ericourt, gave my son, Jesse, a series of piano lessons when he was 18-years-old. As thanks, I gave Daniel and Jayne a dinner party in their honor, but a rude 'wall' guest 'bullied' his way into the limelight that night.

Despite the Frenchman's delightful charm and fame and his lady's stunning beauty and elegance, award winning artist, Sam Wall's oil painting of a Texas Longhorn bull deftly *moo-ved* into the limelight.

Party photographer and my cheery friend, Jayne Laliberte, became bored taking pictures of guests, who only wanted to be snapped in front of Sam's bull, and tried to 'steer' her subjects to another location for 'branding' by her camera. Since Daniel was a great pianist and not a bull fighter, it was no contest. The bull won undisputed honors, serving as the backdrop to most of the conversations and photo-ops of the evening.

Besides dominating most of the 'wall' space, Sam's 4 x 6 framed longhorn hung by

CHAPTER XII

the dinner table to remind guests not to eat like a cow. He wasn't taking any 'bull,' and I continued my search.

The Bull periodically hangs in The River Walk Gallery Co-op in Downtown Washington, a gallery owned and operated by twenty-four of the area's most gifted artists.

I hope Sam's Bull finds an appropriate 'wall-home' in some area Steak House to whet appetites, and remind people what a Texas steer looks like before it lands on your plate.

Kay Currie's Fun

William Lewis is a retired Yankee transplant to Original Washington. Having lived in Philadelphia, he had been a fan of Kay Currie's, when she had worked with the country's first TV station, there. He read in the *Washington Daily News* that Kay was to be the special speaker at the Golden-K breakfast.

CHAPTER XII

"It had to be the same Kay," he reasoned, "because she was going to be speaking about the 'good old days' in radio and TV."

At last, the long lost fan got his chance to meet Kay in person. Since he was able to find Kay, perhaps he could also successfully find that persnickety thingamajig that continues to perplex and confound me so.

By the way, Kay is still extremely glamourous, many moons after her Philly stint. At one time, she even dated one of Elizabeth Taylor's many former husbands. *Yay* for Kay!

Nature's Timing

Dripping rain poured through the Williamston High School Auditorium roof, that evening, splashing into a rather large barrel positioned in the center aisle. The occasion was the **Martin County Player's** production of

CHAPTER XII

The King and I. Mother nature had broken forth with a torrential downpour in the middle of Eva Weatherly-Rosner's expressive Asian dance scene, occurring at the precise moment that her dance led into a pantomime of nature's fury of wind and rain.

Choreographer, Lauren Lukert, instructor at **Farm Life Ballet,** was delighted by the timing of nature's sound effects. Dancer, Eva, was speechless.

Director, Allen Osbourne, says he can recall another time when the sound effects of a summer storm exploded overhead and shook the auditorium at just the right moment during a certain scene, prompting an audience spectator to scratch his head and ask afterwards, "Allen, how in the world did you manage that?"

With Allen's timely touch, I'd be *delighted* to let him manage my beleaguered search!

P. S. The dancer in this story, Eva, comes from a most exciting and creative family. Her maternal grandmother, Vivian Weatherly, is a splendid church organist who still teaches piano lessons at age 85. Her paternal grandmother was a classical ballet dancer, who also danced with The Rockettes at Radio City Music Hall. Eva's mother, Phyllis, is a flautist, organist, pianist and

CHAPTER XII

technical writer. Eva's maternal aunt, Paula Tisdale is a Celtic fiddler, Suzuki Violin teacher and gifted story teller. Who, inside the local loop, can forget Eva's dad? He was the clever fellow in the preface of this book who asked me if my search for the thingamajig was kind of like 'searching for the Holy Grail.' The multitude of his talents equal those of the rest of his family.

Melting pot family

There is another unique family from our town worthy of mentioning. The five grown siblings include a 62-year-old Buddhist monk, Tom Hardison, who is also an accomplished concert pianist. He taught piano in Japan for several decades and has recently moved to the mountains of North Carolina to establish and build a Buddhist monastery. While others may disagree, Tom purports to see no conflict harmonizing the Biblical Jesus with Buddhism.

One of Tom's sisters is a Catholic nun. Another is a Fundamentalist Baptist and organist for her church. Tom's third sister is an active Charismatic Christian. Each of these siblings

CHAPTER XII

were born and reared in no more unusual place than Washington the Original.

When Tom visits his mom, Mrs. Hardison Alligood, he often performs on Zelma Winfield's grand piano. At 96, Mrs. Winfield continues to open her home for musical gatherings.

Stirring up hornet's next

Moons ago, in Enfield, N.C., on a cold wintry day, Sam Davis' brother, J.D., brought a hornets nest home, considering not that its occupants might still be in the nest keeping warm. When the hornets warmed up near the fireplace, they came out to explore their new environment. Everyone in the home dashed outside as quick as lightening. They did not return home until it was as cold in the house as it was outside. Upon their return, the hornets were naturally cuddling together in their nest and J.D. carried it, ever so gingerly, back into the woods.

It wasn't enough that J.D. brought hornets home. Not at all. But on another wintry occasion,

In Search of the Thingamajig...

CHAPTER XII

he accidentally shot a hornet's nest on one of his hunting escapades. This time, the livid hornets made a mad buzz after the culprit and his brother Sam, and friends, forcing them to make a lifesaving dash into an icy cold creek. Sam exclaimed, "They don't give up easily. Those rascally hornets will sting you from now on!"

Telulah

Telulah's a southern gal, who has become rather rude, after having lived in Paris, France, for too many years. Telulah knows that I am her only friend, and she has offered to help me promote the book that you are now reading, even though she thinks that I am no literary genius. She accuses me of being a lousy writer, and to add insult to injury, she's even lambastes the Countess and her exploits.

This feisty 'lady' justifiably accuses me of manipulating her, and must be resigned to her fate, since she is just a puppet. Telulah was created by the artist Mary Whichard for me, a

CHAPTER XII

qualified Ventriloquist, and if Telulah knows what is best for her, she will dismiss her tendency to speak her mind when we perform.

Sandrea and Telulah
A Southern Belle and Jew-ah.
I hope no one will sue-ah;
We only speak what's true-ah.

argain Hunters

If I were a rich woman, I would still shop second hand in my search for thingamajigs. Everything I own is second hand, including my husband, Joe. It must be in my blood to find a bargain, even though the wife of Joe's brief first marriage evidently didn't think so.

The Countess told me that she was shocked to learn that her very wealthy friend from the north, Betsy Bannister, is an addicted bargain hunter at resale shops. (Betsy just came out of the closet on this issue!)

In Search of the Thingamajig...

CHAPTER XII

I volunteered to become a resale tour guide hostess when Betsy visited our town. Betsy and I tried to convert the Countess to our obsession. Betsy told us of the time she received a gift certificate to a fancy exclusive clothing store from a friend who was trying to break her of her needless passion. It upset Betsy so much that she cried at the very idea of buying a new, expensive item, even if it *was* with someone else's money.

Bargains

Some folks call us stingy.
I think they're unkind.
To bargain-hunt we travel far
Until great buys we find.

Food, clothes and jewels, so very neat.
It really is a special treat.
To find the things we want and need.
We know it is a healthy greed.

Rich or Poor

Whether rich or poor
Buying new is a bore.
Second hand we adore.
Third hand we implore.
Fourth hand we explore.
We're no Eva Gabor.

CHAPTER XII

A Busy Bea

This is not the first time my 80-year-young friend, going on thirty, went on a buying spree. She is innocently flirtatious, imaginative and a highly motivated poet, and Bea Seal Simmons is her name. Bea couldn't resist the bargains at Dillard's Outlet Center, when visiting Arlington, Texas. She found the prices better than a resale shop. Liz Claiborne dresses sold for $7, and sweater vests for $3. Bea spent all day on a buying spree, not even concerned about my search. I asked her "What finally stopped your wild buying spree?" She answered, "The store closed on me!"

Bea admitted going back the next day.

The ever so Busy Bea
Went on a wild buying spree.
She bought all she could see,
But not one thing for me.

Bea found bargains galore
And she kept buying more.
They then closed the store,
Forcing Bea out the door!

In Search of the Thingamajig...

CHAPTER XII

Disp'hair

My musician friends, Lil Etchison and her daughter, Jennifer, perform swing music every Thursday at Nicki's Restaurant in Washington's Downtown. They also help out on Starlight Ferry Cruises to help fund-raise. One day, when Lil was not entertaining, she wanted to be as creative with her scissors as she is with her guitar and gave me a French-boy haircut. My extra special aunt-in-law, Lib Ross, exclaimed to me, "Your hairdresser must be after your husband!"

Then my friend, Leroy Carver, shared, "Your haircut would have been a disaster if you did not have the face for it!" When someone asked my husband, "Who cut your wife's hair?" He sadly replied, "What hair?"

To keep from entering disp'hair, I busily searched for the thingamajig and noticed that only half of the people did not like my look. I guess the other half believed my face to be okay enough to handle that French-boy style.

CHAPTER XIII

B ar Mitzvah Bash

I would do almost anything to attend a Bar Mitzvah — that rite of passage which celebrates a Jewish boy's entrance into manhood.

I'd scale the highest mountain, or swim the deepest sea to partake in such an extravaganza. Well, in fact, I recently did just that — spending

In Search of the Thingamajig...

CHAPTER XIII

20 torturous hours driving, bumper to bumper, over Thanksgiving weekend with my 'Joeffeur' at the wheel, three teenagers, and an inquisitive and rambunctious ten-year-old. Believe you me, teenagers should be put to sleep when they turn thirteen, immediately after their 'rite of passage,' and waked up at twenty-one. This would solve a lot of stress-related problems adults have with eager-beaver teeny-boppers.

My Greenville, N.C. friend and historian, Odeda Rosenthal, a Sabra (native born Israeli), whose father was Editor of the Jerusalem Post, says God instills obnoxiousness in teenagers so parents won't be devastated when they are ready to leave home.

But I digress. We Davises survived our adventurous ordeal to and from Squirrel Hill, experiencing on the way a rare view of a double arched rainbow just north of Richmond, Va., loosing our way around Washington, D.C., and, again, at the Monroeville/Pittsburgh exit, where, in the confusion of the moment, we witnessed two splendidly gorgeous specimens of wild

CHAPTER XIII

turkeys, which glided effortlessly in front of our vehicle onto a clearing by the road side.

Mom was sorry we didn't *invite* them (i.e., our two feathered friends) to her Thanksgiving dinner. But it was true she had *company* already (three turkeys, the fix'ns, and plenty of hungry mouths to feed). Two more would have made a 'crowd,' we reasoned!

Holiday-timed bar mitzvahs are occasions to remember the perils of family dynamics. It's great to be with all of the relatives, of course, but there are often enough touchy social logistics to cause one to desire to climb into a hole and hide, or, like my brother, Mike, not to show up at all — which demonstrated to me, once again, his brotherly depth of wisdom!

Usually calm and easy going, I found myself harried beyond belief, while simultaneously anticipating the time of my life at the bar mitzvah. It was a doubled-edged treat.

Our Downtown Pittsburgh hotel was filled to capacity with high school and college marching bands and drill teams from Texas,

CHAPTER XIII

Iowa, and Illinois, all in town for the annual Christmas Parade. In addition, conference tournament volleyball players and fans were staying at the Hotel with us; the Pittsburgh Panther football team was housed there to prepare for their big game with rival West Virginia University at Three Rivers Stadium; plus the sizeable contingent of family were all there, like us, to attend the bar mitzvah.

It was pandemonium! All the bus loads of parade bands seemed to arrive at the same time, filing into the hotel like army ants and lining up a hundred deep for their turn in one of the five elevators going up. We spent forty-five minutes trying to catch an elevator, of all things, making us late for our first bar mitzvah dinner which was held especially for us out-of-towners.

Elevator rage permeated the atmosphere!

Late getting to our party, I caused a scene going back down on the overloaded elevator. "Did you *have* to get out on the 11th floor?" I chided a very tall young woman (probably a volleyball player).

"We're already late enough!"

CHAPTER XIII

My husband took my temporary insanity in stride, sharing with the befuddled elevator riders, "That's a joke. It's supposed to be funny... Lighten up. She thinks she's on a *Seinfeld* set."

The elevator passengers looked nervously at the ceiling, not knowing what to think. ("Who's that lady," I heard someone mumble, as we exited the lobby level?)

I was out of the lift like a shot and already headed for the front door. I didn't want to be any later than I already was to the first of three scheduled mitzvah parties. This was my 'cup of tea,' after all! Besides, I was *searching* in full gear.

After the opening reception, a special bar mitzvah ceremony conducted by a rabbi, a full course meal, and the after-dinner speech-making, the mitzvah guests were eager to get back to the hotel and prepare for the next big day. The trolley driver, however, had other plans for us. Chartered especially for this occasion, he was instructed, unbeknownst to us, to trolley to the top of Mount Washington for a moonlit view of Pittsburgh. But, besides

CHAPTER XIII

being tired, the obvious problem was that we were literally packed into the tour bus like gefulte fish! Not one soul was interested in delaying our return to the hotel. We were 'pooped!' But, evidently, we didn't have a vote! We were literally *hijacked* bar mitzvah guests, like it or not!

It's impossible to deny, Pittsburgh all lit up from atop Mount Washington, was a sight to behold — but not one most of the trolley car out-of-towners had the stomach for, and certainly not at that particular time. In fact, some of us were horrified, with visions of failing breaks, a runaway trolley, people strewn hither and yon down the mountain side, newspaper reports of our demise published around the world — a ready potential for sheer disaster, as we first climbed and then descended that breathtaking, winding mountain highway. (It would have made more sense to have taken the nearby lift up the mountain to sight see. It was practically straight up, too, but not so scary as that trolley ride!)

The grand bar mitzvah dinner/dance was as spectacular as the William Penn Hotel in which it was held. The bar *mitzvahed* boy

CHAPTER XIII

gave a great speech, after being *toasted* by his friends. Afterwards, a special quartet played riveting and spirited Yiddish klezmer music, while the Cleveland-based band, *Special Request*, continued playing 'til midnight, so that we could dance the night (and fat) away — But, for some reason, it (the fat) dissolved not.

When I marveled at my daughter Hannah's swing dancing skills, she said, "I really don't know how I do these dances. I was only faking it." She takes after her daddy. He's a cross-dancer — between Dick van Dyke, Bill Cosby and Gomer Pyle. Some folks think he has the flair of a Fred Astaire.

As opposed, as it was, to our natural instincts, the Davis clan tried to behave. We tried not to cause too much stir at the hotel, where we were domiciled for three nights. But considering our entourage of three teens, our 10-year-old Marriott Menace, and a couple of wacky, over-aged, slightly abused parents, I think we behaved rather civilly for the stresses such a trip entailed.

Pardon the expression, but, like many other guests, we did *our* share of 'pigging out'

CHAPTER XIII

at each of the bar mitzvah events. However, the biggest 'Oy Vey' of this special occasion was when astonished Hannah told me that the kids she ate with were actually served *ham* sandwiches at the children's banquet. 'Surprised' was not the word to most of the kids there, plus those of us who heard about it later. Ham is still considered *unkosher* to observant Jews, which most of the bar mitzvah guests were, and it most definitely wasn't on this particular menu, or we'd all be totally dumb-struck if, per chance, it had been!

    Naturally, I had looked forward to the bright prospect of finding the thingamajig on our bar mitzvah outing. I could have relaxed, alas, and been happy and content, ever after. But, nothing has really changed. Discovery is meticulously slow in coming. So, my orders are still, "forward, march," to continue my search for that elusive *doomaflachee* — the word that Hannah Ruth (along with her good friend, Grace Nicholls) so aptly use to describe it in their various discussions and observations about 'weird Mom's' search.

CHAPTER XIII

n the Passover

We were invited to a Passover Seder while visiting my sister, Sorah, in Tenafly, New Jersey. "Maybe, just maybe," I thought, "the Rabbi has some ideas on helping me find the thingamajig."

Fifteen minutes after we arrived, my 12-year-old daughter, Rebekah, exclaimed to Rabbi Konicoff, "You are a jolly Jew!"

"We should always be joyful and praise God!," he replied.

Two hours later, at ten, the Konicoff family started their second night of the Passover Seder after much preparation. We do this to commemorate the Exodus of the Hebrews from their slavery in Egypt to their wilderness journey and onward to the Promised Land.

Rebekah whispered to me, "The Rabbi is just like Daddy. He never stops talking!"

CHAPTER XIII

Then at Midnight, it was time to eat the matzoh (specially prepared unleavened bread). It's a mitzvah (good deed) to eat matzoh, tradition says. Famished, we all ate enough matzoh to last a lifetime. The matzoh that is eaten on the first night of the Passover represents faith. On the second night it represents health. That's why it's a mitzvah to eat as much matzoh as you can, according to orthodox teaching. We ate it for an hour! No talking. We could only crunch the matzoh with a straight face. May I respectfully suggest that eating all that matzoh is a *mitzvah* to the matzoh makers!

Then, at 1 AM Rebekah said to the Rabbi, "I have two questions, but I want you to answer each one in one minute, not twenty minutes!"

Finally at 3 AM, the meal and the reading of the Passover story ended. I was too exhausted to ask the Rabbi my serious question, "Where can one find the thingamajig?"

By the time we left, we experienced what the Hebrews felt when they finally left Egypt. Freedom!

CHAPTER XIII

Holy Cow!

Podiatrist Dr. James "Bunk" Roberson, farms and raises animals as a hobby. Summers, he distributes farm fresh produce to needy folks.

Wearing my red dress at an elegant wedding reception in Bunk's red walled home, I became privy to the news of his newly born red heifer, whose parents were black haired. I grew so excited thinking my search might soon be ended. Bunk informed me that his heifer was for sale. Flabbergasted, I pleaded, "Don't sell it! Rabbis have been looking for one to breed, in order to have a perfect red one, so that it's ashes can cleanse a rebuilt Temple."

The next day I called the conservative Polish Rabbi in Greenville and reported, "Rabbi, I've found the red heifer!" He replied, "That's *vunderful*! But there is nothing I can do about it."

In Search of the Thingamajig...

CHAPTER XIII

I begged, "But Rabbis in Israel are searching... Please help!"

"That's *their* problem. Have a nice day." Click.

I then contacted the ultra-orthodox Rabbi Herman Posner in Raleigh, and he was delighted to help. I have since learned that red heifers have been found in the Bible Belt and sold to religious authorities in Israel. According to Biblical prophecy, this is one of the many signs which demonstrate that we are in the end times. I hope my search ends before the *end*!

P.S. I learn a great deal about end time prophecy via the **'Midnight Call Magazine,'** and the yearly conventions they sponsor in Myrtle Beach with the top prophecy teachers in the world. Call 800-845-2420, and you, too, can prepare yourself for the prophetic 'Day of the Lord.'

CHAPTER XIII

izpah

The late Mr. Hallett Ward, a prominent lawyer in Original Washington, built and lived in a late Victorian home before 1908. We Davises now own that house, sitting on two acres of land in the center of Washington. Mrs. Norfleet Hodges told me that Hallett named this house, 'Mizpah,' which is a Hebrew word meaning "The Lord watch between you and me, while we are absent one from another." (Genesis 31:49)

Several weeks after learning about Mizpah, my 'archeologist' husband uncovered a heavy marble brick cornerstone, while digging in the yard to plant a shrub. It had the word 'Mizpah' engraved into it.

Little did Mr. Ward know that I would one day dwell in his mansion and would need that Bible verse to help keep me in line, as I search for the thingamajig.

CHAPTER XIII

Hanukkah Crasher!

Several years back, I sponsored a Hanukkah party in my home, in order to share the fun tradition, and it's historical reality. Well, lo and behold, one dressed as Santa had the "chutzpah," meaning audacity, to crash the celebration.

Oy vey! It was John Cantrell, and he sang, "We wish you a merry Hanukkah," and my bouncer husband let him stay.

My mom trained me to believe in Santa until I learned otherwise in the first grade. However, my children were deprived of the excitement of his yearly 'visitations.' Their Aunt Lib was especially dismayed about my lack of Christmas spirit.

The Christmas of '94 was a turning point for me. Returning home from a matinée Christmas concert at the Chocowinity

CHAPTER XIII

Methodist Church, I and all of the Davis Clan saw an incredible image of Santa. As we drove across the bridge into Washington, he was distinctly outlined in a cloud formation.

I shouted, "I can't believe it. It's actually true! He's real after all!" I apologized to the family for me being such a 'stick in the mud' all these years. When we arrived home, we were amazed to see a Christmas tree, (you may call it a Hanukkah bush, if you like), laying in our yard, as if Santa dropped it from that cloud.

It was a perfectly beautiful tree, not the kind of reject that we regularly get the day before Christmas, due to the frugal factor.

Several days later, we discovered who our Santa was that delivered our majestic tree. He was none other than a jolly Dutch artist, Frans Van Baars, co-owner with Brenda, his wife, of Van Baars Waterfront Gallery in Downtown Washington.

That's what I call 'a Dutch treat!'

In Search of the Thingamajig...

CHAPTER XIV

Animal Crackers

Scooter and the Sparrows

Amy Sparrow and her husband, Joe, are owners of Sparrow's General Store in nearby Winsteadville. Their friends, Eileen and David Curtis, were raising a baby otter named Scooter and would bring him over to visit their black lab, Chance. It was love at first sight, as they swam

CHAPTER XIV

together in Jordan Creek. Sometimes a local flock of geese would join in the frolicking.

David asked the Sparrows to care for Scooter during their vacation, and they accepted. Scooter was trained to use the toilet, but when Eileen reported that Scooter usually sleeps with them, Amy's eyes seemed as big as her face. She told Joe that it wouldn't happen in her lifetime!

One should never say never. That night, Amy made Scooter a soft bed with a stuffed toy. Scooter whimpered. Amy moved him into the utility room and Scooter howled! By 1 AM, Amy capitulated. Scooter slid under the covers nestling at her and Joe's feet. Scooter was heard sighing before he promptly fell asleep.

Scooter is now grown and resides in a natural habitat, not deprived of a normal life.

Amy plans to produce a book of her many 'stranger than fiction' animal stories, that she has had published in *The Pamlico Scoop*. The title of her book will be, 'I Slept With An Otter.'

CHAPTER XIV

Tom's Goats

Tom Forbes' first wife got the house. Tom got the goats. So, Tom searched for a second wife, who would love 'kids.'

Tom found and married Irene Glover, a master potter, who, likewise, was a goatherd. They started out with five nanny goats and after sixteen years, they have well over 100.

The most stressful experience for a goatherd comes at kidding time. Tom says, "I pray first, then shout for Irene. She has saved lots of kids and has kept me from failing as a 'Good Shepherd.' The Good Book says to 'Look well to thy herd and know the state of thy flocks.'"

When it is not kidding time, Tom and his identical twin, Ola and their 'kid' brother, Bill, play music and sing in their own country western trio called *The Forbes Brothers*. These are truly amazing guys, worthy of their own book.

CHAPTER XIV

Where, oh where?

My neighbor, Mrs. Buckman, agreed to baby-sit an old dog that belonged to her vacationing daughter. After several days, the dog, Abby, must have tried to find her way back to her master's home in Edenton, North Carolina. A distraught Mrs. Buckman begged me to help her search for Abby in the cold midnight hour.

I never give up my beauty rest, even to search for the thingamajig, but I did agree to this search, since Abby was at the mercy of traffic and the severe night cold. She was blind and deaf at fourteen-years-old. We searched in vain as Mrs. Buckman called out her name. Getting desperate for my sleep, I was relieved when Mrs. Buckman called off the search.

The next day, a lovely lady, Nancy Addiss, heard about the poor missing pooch, and she and her daughter-in-law, Trish, searched for hours on end. They did not give

CHAPTER XIV

up until they finally found Abby, sleeping in the sun on a lawn three blocks away from where she slipped away.

Oh where oh where
Did that old dog go;
Mrs. Buckman's upset.
Searching high and low.

The dog's blind and deaf,
And is very old;
How could she leave?
Not being that bold.

We looked all around.
The dog we did miss;
Mrs. Buckman then called
Sweet Nancy Addiss.

Then Nancy and Trish
Would never give up;
For hours on end
They looked for that pup!

CHAPTER XIV

Christmas Critter

Looking out their kitchen window on a frosty Christmas morning, Linda and Don Clark spotted an animal moving low to the ground, exhaling clouds of freezing breath, in a nearby field. Perplexed, they put on their robes and headed out. The two cautiously approached a rather large creature, which was rooting in a woodpile. The critter looked fearless and hungry. Don and Linda then put out holiday leftovers for their newly discovered and strange-looking 'friend.'

Lingering for several days, the animal made itself cozy bedding in the Clark's yard. With food so generously available, the happy critter maintained his nearby presence. But to Don's dismay, he soon realized that what he had hoped might be 200 pounds of ham, fatback and bacon, a virtual gift sent from above, was actually their neighbor's new thingama-*Pig*, a huge Vietnamese hog, named Suzie. Responding to an add, Suzie's 'parents' were overjoyed that their 'portly pet' was returned before becoming *official* 'breakfast fodder' to the Clark family in the New Year.

CHAPTER XIV

Poochie

In 1989, Poochie (my Aunt's 15-year-old *senior citizen*) flew all the way from Long Island, N.Y., to New Bern's spiffy Jetport for a visit.

Poochie proceeded to have a chronic case of tinkle-itis. Little wonder poor Poochie's master, my beloved Aunt Esther Greenfield, insisted on taking the next flight back with her *accomplice*. It was an expensive two-hour vacation that benefited me not in my search!

Whatever the outcome to my lifelong search, ol' Poochie thought he must have found the object of his *own* search, when, in the process of tinkling, he scented up nearly every corner in my house with his perfume.

I hope that when I find the 'thingy,' it won't be anything like what Poochie found, whatever that was that excited him so. I would be so disappointed, and embarrassed, as well! What was that little dog thinking, anyway?

CHAPTER XIV

Poor 'Deer!'

My book designer, Phyllis Zawislak, known to some as Ms. 'Z,' recently made her mark by developing an extremely 'putrid' formula that keeps hungry deer from munching at will on her plants. A local soy farmer tested this no-name, 'thingamajig-gy' product with positive results.

Ms. Z's Pamlico Plantation residence (located on Broad Creek near Washington) is no longer a regular gathering place for roaming deer. She has outsmarted the confused creatures. Normally adept at breaking and entering almost any obstructions put in their path to devour tasty foliage, these 'poor deers' avoid Z's fenceless plot like the plague, when she sprays.

Her plants, however, *like* the formula. The fertilizer effect invigorates them and promotes healthy growth, while her recipe's pungent scent repels deer with a case of the 'munchies.' It's not what I've been searching for — but it *did* cause a 'stink,' of sorts.

In Search of the Thingamajig...

CHAPTER XV

Bath 'n Bath in Bath

Pianist, Dr. Charles Bath from adjacent Greenville, with his wife, violinist Joanne Bath, serenaded a small crowd in Bath, the oldest town in North Carolina. Bath Towne is located only 15 minutes east of Washington.

The Baths donated their talents for the renovation project of the oldest North Carolina

CHAPTER XV

church, St. Thomas Episcopal. I was hoping my quest would end there, but it did not. However, a poem was birthed in my mind as a result of my presence at their inspiring concert.

> *Bath 'n Bath played in Bath,*
> *That quaint historic town.*
> *They played for free to renovate*
> *St. Thomas; it is run down.*
>
> *Joanne Bath on violin*
> *And Charles on piano*
> *With music to uplift your soul*
> *They played a great 'concerto.'*

Hilton Head

Surely, I thought, I would be able to find the thingamajig on the Island of Hilton Head. The opportunity arose when my son, Jesse, was accepted at the Hilton Head Island International Piano Competition held there each winter.

In Search of the Thingamajig...

CHAPTER XV

Just three of the twenty pianists who survived the competition were native born Americans, with seventeen others being of foreign birth. Not one of them had a clue as to what my search was all about, but nevertheless, I enjoyed every minute of this marvelous occasion. The Competition is open and the islanders are quite supportive. The 2,000 seat auditorium at the Presbyterian Church was filled to capacity for much of the two-day event.

The host family for Jesse was the Brouillards. Mom Eileen just knew redheaded Jesse was a Godsend, since she also has red hair. Much to her delight, people mistook her as his mom — which she was, for a weekend.

CHAPTER XV

Tapp'n with Clicquot

My eldest son, Jesse, brought home his college friend, Jerry, a tap dancer and classically trained African-American actor from Miami. He entertained us with Shakespearian Sonnets, but couldn't help me in my search.

While Jesse was practicing Chopin in the living room, Jerry was tap dancin' to 'Bugle Boy' on the kitchen floor. Two of Jerry's tap dancing buddies are tapping on Broadway in the award winning play, 'Bring in the Noise, Bring in the Funk.' Jerry fit right into our madhouse and even started calling me 'mummy.'

Then, Jerry agreed to be the moderator for our *HATsteria Fashion Show*, with hats designed by African-American Pastor James Long, to support his 'Awake Hour Ministries.' The Countess lobbied to be the only model saying, "I want to be seen wearing all of those beautiful hats!"

CHAPTER XV

Twilah Sisters

Virginia and Twilah are sisters, women of color, each standing nearly six feet tall and fairly wide. They have short bleached blonde hair and are stunning in appearance. When they walk into a crowded room, all eyes gravitate toward their majestic presence.

Virginia plays the piano by ear and accompanies Twilah and herself, singing heavenly harmonies of praise and King David's psalms of thanksgiving. Their powerful voices never need a mike. The sisters live in nearby Williamston and are originally from Altoona, Pennsylvania.

Twilah used to record and sing professionally and is now a health care worker, while Virginia is full-time in the music ministry.

When I heard them sing, I felt I had found the 'thingy' that I was looking for. I wanted to manage and dub them, 'The Twilah Belles.'

CHAPTER XV

Jitterbug

Leroy and Phyllis Carver do not have time to jitterbug, because Phyllis is a bibliophile and a folk musician who sings harmony and accompanies her daughter, the singer/songwriter Linda Clark. Leroy is mighty busy too, as our town's self styled nutritional counselor and Conspiracy Theorist. His goal is to educate everybody who dares to cross his path. But their friends, James and Ann Ellis, from Bayview, had time to dance. They jitterbugged their way through fifty plus years of marriage. However, James has become rather jitterbug-less, lately.

Ann was recently recruited to teach dance by the students at Pantego Elementary School. They were anxious to learn 'real' dancing that is *'nastiless'* and fun. Ann's dance partner became Dr. Cherry, the principal of the school. He is a 65-year-old man, 6'4," and weighs 250 pounds. Ann is a petite and sweet, 5'2," an eyes-are-blue type of gal. The students

CHAPTER XV

loved 'Granny Annie' and doing the Jitterbug, Camel Walk, and Boogie Woogie. I would think that Ann could be of tremendous help to me in my search. "Go Granny, go Granny, go Granny, go."

Funtastic is Ann,
A lady of praise.
She's turning Bath Towne
Into a Jitterbug craze.

She plays drums and spoons.
What more can she do?
She clowns at the hospital,
When sick folks are blue.

With vivacious joy
She spreads the good news.
Worries not what some think
With their don't's and their do's.

So look out for Ann.
She may come your way,
To give you a lift
And brighten your day!

CHAPTER XV

be's Clone

Jan Hasty-Paysour, master gourd artist, musician and owner of 'The Gourd Patch' in Belhaven, was playing and singing 'Dixie' at a gathering at my home. David Jennings, historian, was waiting to perform in costume as Abraham Lincoln. Thinking 'Dixie' might upset Lincoln, Jan found out differently. 'Dixie' was one of President Lincoln's favorite songs.

If I believed in reincarnation, I would think that David Jennings used to be Abe.

David is an expert historian on the Civil War, Native American Culture, World War II from the Allies and the Nazi perspectives and the Holocaust. He has many artifacts to show folks as he shares his knowledge in the schools and for civic groups. Someone like David should certainly be able to help me in my belabored search for the thingamajig.

But, alas, my patience is growing thin.

In Search of the Thingamajig...

CHAPTER XV

Bob London's 'Rolling Trolls'

My innovative friend, Carolyn Ganley, assisted in decorating the Truman private quarters of the White House when she was but 17-years-old. Bess Truman handed down her daughter, Margaret's, formal dresses to Carolyn through Harry's Administrative Assistant, Rose Conway. Only my readers are now privy to these transactions, so keep this historical tidbit to yourself. Carolyn has tried to keep this *hush-hush* all these many years.

Due to this unique experience along with Carolyn's numerous other credentials, I asked her to aid me in my quest for the thingamajig. I felt the two of us might finally get the job done. It certainly wouldn't hurt, at this stage, to try.

So, Carolyn and I drove 75 miles to the *Beaufort Music Festival* in the seaside resort village

CHAPTER XV

by that name. We became awestruck at the sight and sounds of one, *Bob London and His Rolling Trolls One Man Band.*

His act originated, you guessed it, in England's blimey old London Towne. He was the real deal, for sure! My heart leaped. I was elated!

The extraordinary homemade *gizzmo*, adorned with a variety of smirking trolls, was strapped to his back and made me think, "I had finally found my long sought after thingamajig!" (Bob, with his instrument, is pictured on the front cover of this book).

During his break, I asked Bob if he would come to Washington and demonstrate to folks down our way his rare do-hicky.

He accepted. Eureka! Have I found the answer to my tenacious and arduous search, at last? Eyes would have to behold what this man carried on his back and performed with his whole body. Indeed, it was a *thingamajig*, if ever I spied one! In fact, it was one better — a *Thingama-Bob* — in *real* time!

CHAPTER XV

In the months that ensued, Bob performed many times for the young and old alike, on our front porch, in cafes, in concert halls, on various waterfronts, at street festivals — anywhere people wished to congregate. He treated them to the sounds and rhythms of a genuine *thingamajig* with the folk-rock hits of Bob Dylan, The Beatles, The Dooby Brothers, and the likes. Bob knew and performed hundreds of such songs.

London Bob was like the man who came to dinner, and stayed. For nine months he made his home in our backyard in his 1964 renovated Dodge bookmobile, complete with a broadside painting of Dino the Dinosaur. Despite being entertained by his performances, and thinking he looked and talked like the Crocodile Dundee character, my kids began turning sour toward this British invasion. They cherish their 'space' and their teenish fancy was *embarrassed* by Bob and his fanciful gizzmo.

After a farewell party for Bob at the Curiosity Cafe and Coffee Shoppe in Washington, he drove his 'Dino'mobile out West to seek fame and fortune. After registering a visit with family in Arizona, who had preceded

CHAPTER XV

him to America, he drove on to California where he aspired to be discovered.

Through all this, Beaufort County Hospital Administrator, Kenneth Ragland, and wife Sharon, past co-owners of the Curiosity Cafe, were on a business trip to San Diego. As the Raglands were driving down the many roads, Sharon shouted, "Stop the car! There's Bob!" He was sitting outside a West Coast coffee shop, sipping a coffee latté, just as he had spent countless hours doing back in Washington at the Curiosity Cafe and Coffee Shoppe. It was the same old Bob!

Amazed, they exchanged hugs, caught up on the news, and drank more coffee latté.

At last report, Bob is still out West. But I surmise this much: That while his creation and music machine is worthy of 'thingamajig-hood in the thirty-third degree,' it's still 'no cigar.' Rather, I'm afraid that the intrigue of my search may have been dealt a mortal blow. My search will never be the same, after coming so close to finding the object in my obsessive dream.

CHAPTER XV

In the Commode?

Delores Morgan from Bath, gets hysterical with her occasional sidekick, Ann Ellis, before they ever get on stage to entertain. I follow their careers in hopes of discovering a thingamajig or two. One time I caught them backstage hysterically laughing about Ann's wet overalls. Ann is seventy-something, and it was her first time wearing such a garment, and she knew not how to manage them when nature called. The straps got soaked in the commode!

Soon Delores entered the stage, plopped down on the piano stool and began playing. Halfway through Rachmaninoff, she suddenly stopped and exclaimed, "Now I'm going home!" And she began to *boogie woogie*, with Ann, accompanying her on the drums.

Ann's wet straps went unnoticed by the audience, which consisted of Washington's Mother of Mercy Moms and Pops' Club members. They were driven to laughter by Delores' original song,"A Hog Killin' Collard Christmas."

CHAPTER XV

I now take you back to the wet straps, and, possibly, a conclusion to my surprising and unpredictable search. Alas, is the *jig* up?

Straps in the commode,
But nobody know'd;
Where e'er they may be
There's hilarity.
I'm the biggest fan
Of Delores and Ann.
They surely entertain
And yes, they isn't sane.
I follow their career
Will a thingamajig appear?
I guess it doesn't matter
It's just a bunch of **chatter.**

Chatter.... Why, of course. The *jig is* up! After all is said and done, the *jig* is this little volume and it's 'bunch of chatter.' As wise Norfleet Hodges, my confidant, friend, and neighbor, confided in me, "Sandrea, you are the chatterbox, the Master of Chatter, who compiled all this chitchat during your long and serendipitous search. The contents of this book is, most definitely, the *thingamajig* you've been seeking! It was hiding in you all along."

Alas, I rest my case. My meandering search for 'peace of mind' and that 'special something' has found its conclusion — at least, for now.

In Search of the Thingamajig...

ADDENDUM — XVI

SKETCHING
the
SEARCH

Sketches by Tony A. Weichel
Addendum Design by W. Joe Davis

Gotta go to the Spa!

"Grandma Betty begs son-in-law, 'Let my daughter go'!"

ADDENDUM — XVI

Off to the Spa to Meet My Ma!

"Hold that Amtrak!"

Miracle in Catskills

"Close call, Marty!"

In Search of the Thingamajig...

ADDENDUM — XVI

In Search of the Thingamajig...

ADDENDUM — XVI

Witchell's Woes

"Help! Le'me oughta here!"

Thingama-Pow-wow!

"Pow-wow-ing with Chief Grandfather Raven."

ADDENDUM — XVI

The COUNTESS!

"Hunting mushrooms."

"Flaunting her attire."

Abusive woman!
The Countess pulls Publisher's beard at Fu Sun!

In Search of the Thingamajig...

In Search of the Thingamajig...

ADDENDUM — XVI

FRIENDS, ALL...

Tony explains his 'time table.'

Thief!

"Sandrea stealing words from magazine rack."

Ginny serves up a 'scoop' of ice cream at Pamlico Provisions.

ADDENDUM — XVI

In Search of the Thingamajig...

NOTES

In Search of the Thingamajig...

e-mail: www.scoop@skantech.com

In Search of the "T"

CALL 1-800-684-5457 (3831)
1-252-946-1553 / fax 1-252-946-5599

Published by

Funnier Than Fiction Press
1110 1/2 N. Market Street, P. O. Box 1607
Washington, NC 27889

In the Bible Belt and Beyond

e-mail: www.scoop@skantech.com

TO ORDER:

CALL 1-800-684-5457 (3831)
1-252-946-1553 / fax 1-252-946-5599

Book _____ Qty. at $9.95 each $_____

NC residents add 6% sales tax $_____

Postage & Handling $__**3.00**__

Total $_____
  (Cash, Money Order, Check — Only)

Name: _____

Address: _____

City: _____

State: _____

Zip: _____

Home Phone (____)_____

Signature: _____

Funnier Than Fiction Press
1110 1/2 N. Market Street, P. O. Box 1607
Washington, NC 27889